PRENTICE HALL LITERATURE

PENGUIN EDITION

Teaching Resources

Unit 2
A Nation Is Born

The American Experience

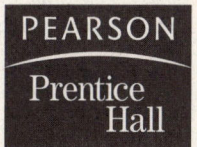

PEARSON
Prentice Hall

Upper Saddle River, New Jersey
Boston, Massachusetts

Copyright © by Pearson Education, Inc., publishing as Pearson Prentice Hall, Upper Saddle River, New Jersey 07458. All rights reserved. Printed in the United States of America. This publication is protected by copyright, and permission should be obtained from the publisher prior to any prohibited reproduction, storage in a retrieval system, or transmission in any form or by any means, electronic, mechanical, photocopying, recording, or likewise. The publisher hereby grants permission to reproduce these pages, in part or in whole, for classroom use only, the number not to exceed the number of students in each class. Notice of copyright must appear on all copies. For information regarding permission(s), write to: Rights and Permissions Department.

ISBN 0-13-165197-8

1 2 3 4 5 6 7 8 9 10   09 08 07 06 05

Contents

UNIT 2

Unit Map 1

Diagnostic Test 2 2

Unit Introduction: Names and Terms to Know 5

Unit Introduction: Focus Questions 6

**from *The Autobiography* and from *Poor Richard's Almanack*
by Benjamin Franklin**
- Vocabulary and Reading Warm-ups 7
- Literary Analysis: Autobiography 11
- Reading Strategy: Drawing Conclusions 12
- Vocabulary Builder 13
- Grammar and Style: Pronoun Case 14
- Support for Writing Lesson 15
- Support for Extend Your Learning 16
- Enrichment: Multiple Careers 17
- Selection Test A 18
- Selection Test B 21
- From the Scholar's Desk: William L. Andrews 24
- Listening and Viewing: William L. Andrews 25

**from *The Interesting Narrative of the Life of Olaudah Equiano*
by Olaudah Equiano**
- Vocabulary and Reading Warm-ups 26
- Literary Analysis: Slave Narratives 30
- Reading Strategy: Summarizing 31
- Vocabulary Builder 32
- Grammar and Style: Active and Passive Voice 33
- Support for Writing Lesson 34
- Support for Extend Your Learning 35
- Enrichment: Film Portrayals of the Slave Trade 36
- Selection Test A 37
- Selection Test B 40

The Declaration of Independence by Thomas Jefferson
from *The Crisis, Number 1,* by Thomas Paine

- Vocabulary and Reading Warm-ups 43
- Literary Analysis: Persuasion 47
- Reading Strategy: Recognizing Changed Words 48
- Vocabulary Builder 49
- Grammar and Style: Parallelism 50
- Support for Writing Lesson 51
- Support for Extend Your Learning 52
- Enrichment: Local Newspaper Editorial 53
- Selection Test A 54
- Selection Test B 57

"An Hymn to the Evening" and "To His Excellency, General Washington"
by Phillis Wheatley

- Vocabulary and Reading Warm-ups 60
- Literary Analysis: Persuasion 64
- Reading Strategy: Clarifying Meaning 65
- Vocabulary Builder 66
- Grammar and Style: Subject and Verb Agreement 67
- Support for Writing Lesson 68
- Support for Extend Your Learning 69
- Enrichment: Fine Art 70
- Selection Test A 71
- Selection Test B 74

"Speech in the Virginia Convention" by Patrick Henry
"Speech in the Convention" by Benjamin Franklin

- Vocabulary and Reading Warm-ups 77
- Literary Analysis: Speeches 81
- Reading Strategy: Evaluating Persuasive Appeals 82
- Vocabulary Builder 83
- Grammar and Style: Double Negatives 84
- Support for Writing Lesson 85
- Support for Extend Your Learning 86
- Enrichment: Persuasion 87
- Selection Test A 88
- Selection Test B 91

"Letter to Her Daughter from the New White House" by Abigail Adams

from *Letters from an American Farmer* by Michel-Guillaume Jean de Crèvecoeur

    Vocabulary and Reading Warm-ups 94

    Literary Analysis: Private and Public Letters (Epistles) 98

    Reading Strategy: Distinguishing Between Fact and Opinion 99

    Vocabulary Builder 100

    Grammar and Style: Semicolons 101

    Support for Writing Lesson 102

    Support for Extend Your Learning 103

    Enrichment: Writing a Business Letter 104

    Selection Test A 105

    Selection Test B 108

Writing About Literature: Analytic Essay: Evaluate Literary Themes 111

Writing About Literature: Replacing Vague Adjectives 112

Writing Workshop: Persuasion: Persuasive Essay 113

Writing Workshop Create Effective Parallelism 114

Spelling: Proofreading Practice 115

Communications Workshop: Analyze Persuasive Techniques 116

Suggestions for Further Reading 117

Benchmark Test 2 118

Answers 124

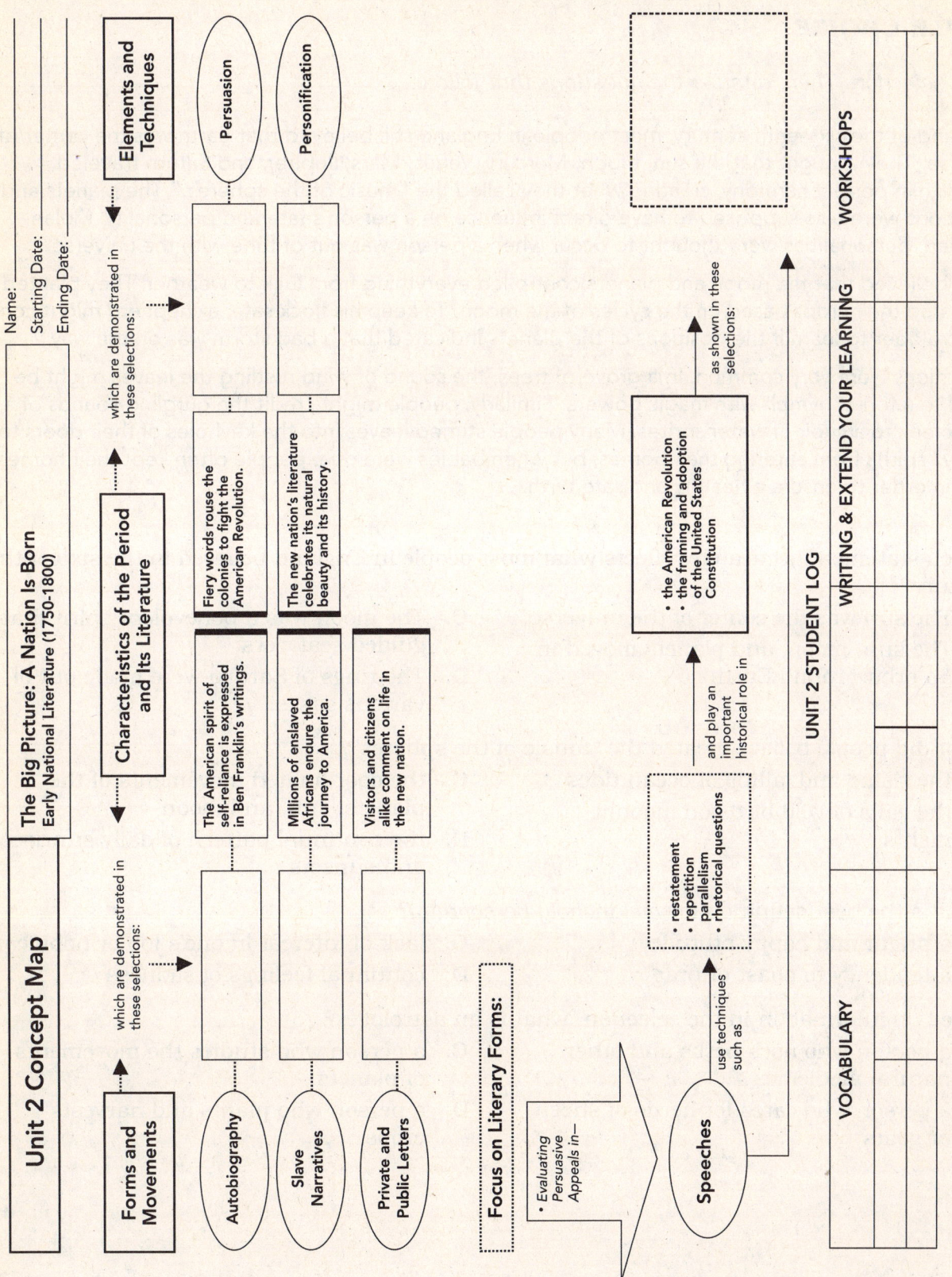

Name _____ Date _____

Unit 2: A Nation Is Born
Diagnostic Test 2

MULTIPLE CHOICE

Read the selection. Then, answer the questions that follow.

At the end of the sixteenth century, most people in England still believed that Earth was the center of the universe. They thought that the sun, moon, Mercury, Venus, Mars, Jupiter, and Saturn traveled around Earth in perfect harmony, creating what they called the "music of the spheres." The planets and their positions were also supposed to have direct influence on a person's fate and personality. Melancholy, or sad, personalities were thought to occur when a person was out of tune with the universe.

People believed that the moon and planets controlled everything from luck to weather. They planted and harvested their crops based on the cycles of the moon. To keep his flock safe, a shepherd might consult an astrologer to learn if the positions of the planets indicated that a bad storm was on the way.

Superstitions were very common. In a grove of trees, the sound of wind rustling the leaves might be attributed to a forest nymph with magic powers. Similarly, people might credit the gurgling sounds of a bubbling creek to a choir of water sprites. Many people stuffed leaves into the keyholes of their doors to prevent evil spirits from entering their homes, but when babies were due, people often kept their homes unlocked in order to ensure a healthy and safe birth.

1. Which statement accurately reflects what most people in England believed in the sixteenth century?
    A. The sun was the center of the universe.
    B. The sun, moon, and planets moved in an orbit around Earth.
    C. The moon was a benevolent spirit that guided seafarers.
    D. The rings of Saturn were made out of various gases.

2. What did people believe created the "music of the spheres"?
    A. the rising and falling of ocean tides
    B. the calls of wild birds on moonlit nights
    C. the coordinated movements of the planets, sun, and moon
    D. the continual pattern of daily sunrises and sunsets

3. What is the best definition for *melancholy personality*?
    A. a bright and happy attitude
    B. a tendency to boast or brag
    C. lack of interest in one's job or hobbies
    D. continual feelings of sadness

4. Based on information in the selection, what is an astrologer?
    A. a person who uses herbs and other natural medicines
    B. a person who cares for herds of sheep or goats
    C. a person who studies the movements of planets
    D. a person who plants and harvests crops

5. According to the passage, what do nymphs and sprites have in common?
   A. They are magical, imaginary characters.
   B. They are elves who live under the surface of lakes and streams.
   C. They are magical characters who live in dark forests.
   D. They are evil and mischievous imaginary characters.

6. What did people often do to protect themselves from evil spirits?
   A. plant crops based on the cycles of the moon
   B. consult astrologers
   C. stuff leaves into the keyholes of their doors
   D. try to travel in perfect harmony

7. What superstition led people to keep their homes unlocked?
   A. They believed it would help their babies have safe births.
   B. They believed it would encourage kind spirits to bless their homes.
   C. They believed it would keep their sheep safe from wolves and dangerous storms.
   D. They believed it would help lonely travelers find comfort and peace.

Read the selection. Then, answer the questions that follow.

Most people recognize the red rose as a symbol of romantic love, but few people realize that flowers and herbs have been used for centuries to convey many different emotions. The Victorians even published books on what they called the "language of flowers." Various plants helped them to express feelings that otherwise seemed too passionate to be conveyed through direct statements. The nuances of this "language" are now mostly forgotten, but some remain. For example, people often give bouquets of white roses to convey messages of honesty or virtue, while yellow roses stand for friendship. Lilies often appear in wedding arrangements and bridal bouquets because these flowers suggest purity and innocence. Someone might place a bouquet of rosemary on the grave of a loved one to send the message *I will always remember you.* Similarly, if someone sends you a bouquet of pansies, the message is *I'm thinking of you.*

Historically, the way people presented flowers to each other also conveyed definite messages. A hopeful suitor might present to his loved one a rosebud with leaves and thorns, conveying the message *I fear, but I hope.* However, if the loved one returned a similar rosebud stem first, the message would be discouraging. This time, it would be *You must neither fear nor hope.* In other words, the answer would be *No thanks!*

8. To many people, what does a red rose symbolize?
   A. honesty or virtue
   B. pride
   C. jealousy or envy
   D. romance

9. Why did people in the Victorian age use plants to express deep feelings and emotions?
   A. Most people could not read and write, so written messages were rare.
   B. Many people believed that it was wrong or too daring to express their feelings directly.
   C. Queen Victoria encouraged her subjects to create formal gardens.
   D. People had trouble communicating with words because of the many different languages.

Name _____ Date _____

10. Which type of flower traditionally represents friendship?
    A. white daisies
    B. white roses
    C. yellow daffodils
    D. yellow roses

11. Why are lilies often used as wedding flowers?
    A. to emphasize the beauty of the bride
    B. to emphasize the wealth and social rank of the bride's family
    C. to emphasize the purity and innocence of the bride
    D. to emphasize the romantic love of the bride and groom

12. Which plant is the symbol of happy and longstanding memories?
    A. rosemary
    B. hyacinth
    C. zinnia
    D. tarragon

13. Which of the following is the most probable reason a man might send a woman some pansies?
    A. to say "I love you"
    B. to say "I miss you"
    C. to say "I am eager to see you again soon"
    D. to say "I am thinking about you"

14. Why might a hopeful suitor want to send his loved one the message *I fear, but I hope*?
    A. to express his wish to marry her
    B. to show that he is uncertain, but hopeful, that she will accept his love
    C. to show that he is afraid that another man might win her love
    D. to express his wish to end the relationship and move on to happier, more hopeful times

15. According to the selection, how might someone use flowers to discourage a suitor from pursuing a relationship?
    A. refuse to accept the suitor's gift of flowers
    B. return the suitor's bouquet with a written note of denial
    C. return a rosebud, with the stem broken in half
    D. return a rosebud, with the stem facing toward the suitor

Unit 2 Resources: A Nation Is Born
© Pearson Education, Inc., publishing as Pearson Prentice Hall. All rights reserved.

Name _____ Date _____

Unit 2 Introduction
Names and Terms to Know

A. DIRECTIONS: *Match each name or term on the left with its fact on the right. Write the letter of the fact on the line before the name or term it defines.*

Names and Terms

___ 1. Enlightenment

___ 2. The American Revolution

___ 3. Constitution

___ 4. Bill of Rights

___ 5. Declaration of Independence

___ 6. Thomas Jefferson

___ 7. Thomas Paine

___ 8. *The Federalist*

___ 9. Phillis Wheatley

Facts

A. a document that formed the nation's political foundation; written in 1787 and ratified after extended controversy

B. person who wrote *Common Sense*, an appeale to reason to gather support for fighting for independence

C. statement of the growing need for independence, including accusations against King George III; written by Thomas Jefferson, Benjamin Franklin, and others

D. war that began as a result of the colonies' growing need for independence and the increase in British restrictions

E. essays written by Alexander Hamilton, John Jay, and James Madison that discussed principles of American government

F. person who showed early literary ability while a young slave; published poems in England

G. document added to the Constitution to reassure people that centralized power would not limit their individual rights

H. aperiod of intellectual development

I. person who drafted the Declaration of Independence; served as president

B. DIRECTIONS: *Write an additional fact about each of the following names and terms.*

1. Enlightenment: _____
2. American Revolution: _____
   _____
3. Constitution: _____
   _____
4. *The Federalist:* _____
   _____

Name _____ Date _____

Unit 2 Introduction
Focus Questions

DIRECTIONS: *Use the hints below to help you answer the Focus Questions. You will find all of the information in the Unit Introduction in your textbook.*

1. What series of events set the stage for war between the American colonies and the British?
   Hint: What event caused the British government to look to the colonists for increased funds? _____
   _____
   _____

   Hint: What were the measures taken by the British government to raise money? _____
   _____
   _____

2. What challenges did the new country face in its quest for self-government?
   Hint: Which documents were drafted by the new nation? _____
   _____
   _____

   Hint: What issues were the leaders of the new nation trying to address? _____
   _____
   _____

3. In what ways did politics influence literature during this period?
   Hint: Think about the kinds of literature that could be easily spread from one place to another. _____
   _____
   _____

   Hint: Think about the backgrounds of some of the people who would have been writing during this period. _____
   _____
   _____

from **The Autobiography** and *from* **Poor Richard's Almanack** by Benjamin Franklin

Vocabulary Warm-up Word Lists

Study these words from the selections. Then, complete the activities.

Word List A

conferred [kon FURD] *v.* gave; assigned
  They <u>conferred</u> the highest honor on their hero.

enumerations [ee noo mer AY shuns] *n.* lists; countings
  This book has <u>enumerations</u> of the rulers of the countries.

eradicate [ee RAD uh kayt] *v.* root out; destroy totally
  We are trying to <u>eradicate</u> all the causes of the problem.

faulty [FAWL tee] *adj.* having faults; imperfect
  Building with <u>faulty</u> materials caused the damage.

posterity [pos TAIR uh tee] *n.* future generations
  She donated her collection for the benefit of <u>posterity</u>.

practicable [PRAK tik uh bl] *adj.* doable; usable
  Your plan sounds great, but it is not <u>practicable</u>.

relapses [REE lap sez] *n.* falls back into illness or habits
  We seemed cured, but we all had <u>relapses</u> of the disease.

trifling [TRY fling] *adj.* unimportant; trivial
  Don't bother me now with such <u>trifling</u> matters.

Word List B

allotted [uh LOT ed] *v.* gave a share; distributed
  The producer <u>allotted</u> each performer three minutes.

autobiography [aw toh by OG re fee] *n.* self-written life story
  In my <u>autobiography</u>, I will give all the details no one knows.

benevolent [ben EH voh lent] *adj.* generous; charitable
  His contributions show him to be a <u>benevolent</u> millionaire.

incorrigible [in KOR ij uh bl] *adj.* not correctable
  She is <u>incorrigible</u> and will not change her bad habits.

sensibly [SEN sib lee] *adv.* with feeling; with good sense
  In a crisis, stay in control and act <u>sensibly</u>.

speculative [SPEK yoo la tiv] *adj.* possible but not proved
  We try not to accept <u>speculative</u> notions as historical fact.

subsequent [SUB se kwent] *adj.* following; next
  <u>Subsequent</u> events proved that our prediction was correct.

unremitting [un ree MIT ing] *adj.* not letting up; relentless
  The <u>unremitting</u> boos of the crowd did not disturb him.

Name _____ Date _____

from The Autobiography and from Poor Richard's Almanack by Benjamin Franklin
Vocabulary Warm-up Exercises

Exercise A *Fill in the blanks, using each word from Word List A only once.*

The land that sloped down gently behind the colonial church was a cemetery. By taking such good care of the site, the town had [1] _____ great honor on the men, women, and children who had died during an eighteenth-century epidemic. Many of the worn, gray headstones gave [2] _____ of the deeds of the deceased, and some markers listed their [3] _____ for several generations. Most of these colonists had fallen to a disease that medical science has since been able to [4] _____. In those days, however, attacks and [5] _____ were often fatal. Even a head cold was not a [6] _____ matter. Doctors were scarce, and home remedies were [7] _____. People did all that was [8] _____, but the cemetery was proof that their efforts were far from successful.

Exercise B *Answer the questions with complete explanations.*

1. If an artist publishes her <u>autobiography</u>, who wrote it for her?
   _____

2. If a witness gives a <u>speculative</u> account of an event, is the witness guessing at what might have happened?
   _____

3. If you dress <u>sensibly</u>, are your clothes appropriate for the occasion?
   _____

4. If every group is <u>allotted</u> twenty seats, are the seats distributed equally?
   _____

5. If you bought a radio and received a <u>subsequent</u> bill, when did you receive the bill?
   _____

6. If you praise a <u>benevolent</u> woman, what kind of actions might you be praising her for?
   _____

7. If an enemy's attack is <u>unremitting</u>, when does it grow weaker?
   _____

8. If a man describes himself as an <u>incorrigible</u> coward, when does he plan to stop being a coward?
   _____

Name _____ Date _____

from The Autobiography and from Poor Richard's Almanack by Benjamin Franklin
Reading Warm-up A

Read the following passage. Pay special attention to the underlined words. Then, read it again, and complete the activities. Use a separate sheet of paper for your written answers.

An almanac is a book of useful and useless information, ranging from the essential to the trifling. It usually contains such things as sunrise times, phases of the moon, tides, and weather predictions. It may also include enumerations of geographical facts and lists of statistics, advice on farming, sayings, tales, and other entertaining reading. Archaeologists have found almanacs in the ruins of ancient civilizations, including the Chinese and the Aztec. Colonists brought almanacs to the New World. In fact, the first book published in British North America was an almanac printed in 1639.

During the 1700s, almanacs developed into a form of folk literature. They gradually added more stories, anecdotes, jokes, and poetry. Almanacs tried to reach as many people as possible in a land where so many different languages were spoken. To make this goal practicable, almanacs were published in a great variety of languages. There were almanacs in Cherokee, Chippewa, Delaware, Dutch, German, Hebrew, Swedish, Russian, Polish, and Italian.

One event conferred a unique legal honor on almanacs and gave them increased status. According to court records, a young Illinois attorney named Abraham Lincoln actually won a case by using a *Farmer's Almanac*. A witness said he had seen a murder by moonlight. Lincoln proved that the witness's testimony was faulty. He produced an almanac that showed that, on the night in question, only a sliver of a moon shone, not enough for the witness to have seen the crime.

Popular almanac features included advice on how to eradicate certain pests from the land, completely eliminating these destructive insects. Almanacs also included health remedies to cure diseases and prevent relapses so that people did not get sick again. Posterity has not kept the faith in almanacs that previous generations had, but we do still find them entertaining.

1. Circle the word that means the opposite of *trifling*. Describe a *trifling* experience you have had.

2. Circle the word that means the same as *enumerations*. What *enumerations* might you find in a school yearbook?

3. Underline the words that tell what made reaching many people *practicable*. Describe something that is not *practicable*.

4. Circle the word that means the same as *conferred*. Name an honor that has been *conferred* on someone.

5. Underline the words that tell why the testimony was *faulty*. Describe a time you used a *faulty* product.

6. Circle the words that explain *eradicate*. Name something people should *eradicate*.

7. Underline the words that explain *relapses*. Use *relapses* in a sentence.

8. Circle the words that help explain *posterity*. Define *posterity* in your own words.

Unit 2 Resources: A Nation Is Born
© Pearson Education, Inc., publishing as Pearson Prentice Hall. All rights reserved.

Name _____ Date _____

from The Autobiography and *from* Poor Richard's Almanack by Benjamin Franklin
Reading Warm-up B

Read the following passage. Pay special attention to the underlined words. Then, read it again, and complete the activities. Use a separate sheet of paper for your written answers.

The craft of autobiography is an underappreciated literary skill. Writing the story of one's own life requires art and discipline, sensitivity and control, demanding the ability to identify meaningful experiences and relate them clearly and sensibly, with the perfect combination of passion and reason. The best autobiographies are a satisfying blend of subjectivity and objectivity.

A good autobiography is the act of rendering your own life in words, an act that takes imagination or, as one memoirist calls it, the act of "inventing the truth." An autobiography is much more extensive than a memoir, which focuses on some segment of a life, while an autobiography traverses a whole life from birth to the present. In an autobiography, the more significant events are usually allotted more space, assigned more pages, and nothing genuinely important is omitted. Of course an autobiography has a personal point of view, but fact and truth are essential; merely speculative statements are of little use. After all, the writer should know what really happened and relate it.

People write autobiographies for different reasons. Some write to chronicle their unremitting struggles to overcome wave after wave of opposition; some write to justify their notorious acts; some write to understand or interpret the past; some write to establish an identity. Some autobiographers portray themselves as finer than they really were—more elegant and intelligent, more generous and benevolent, more loving and sympathetic; some portray themselves as worse—more selfish and cynical, more stubborn and even incorrigible.

Every autobiography is a version of the truth. If the writer has at least attempted to be honest, books that come later will reveal that honesty and show it in the best light. Such subsequent biographies and studies often confer more honor, praise, and renown on autobiographers than they can possibly confer on themselves.

1. Underline the words that define autobiography. Name an *autobiography* you have read or would like to read.

2. Circle the words that help explain sensibly. Use *sensibly* in a sentence.

3. Underline the word that means the same as allotted. How much time are you *allotted* for English class?

4. Circle the words that mean "not speculative." When might *speculative* statements be useful?

5. Underline the words that help explain unremitting. Name a synonym for *unremitting*.

6. Circle the word that means about the same as benevolent. Describe an action you would consider *benevolent*.

7. Circle the word that means about the same as incorrigible. Use *incorrigible* in a sentence of your own.

8. Underline the words that explain subsequent. Name something you plan to do *subsequent* to finishing this assignment.

Unit 2 Resources: A Nation Is Born
© Pearson Education, Inc., publishing as Pearson Prentice Hall. All rights reserved.

Name _____ Date _____

from **The Autobiography** and from **Poor Richard's Almanack** by Benjamin Franklin
Literary Analysis: Autobiography

An **autobiography** is a person's written account of his or her own life. Though by its nature subjective, it nevertheless offers valuable insight into the author's personality, thoughts, and feelings.

DIRECTIONS: *Read these passages from* The Autobiography. *Then, on the lines provided, sum up what they reveal about Franklin's attitudes and personality.*

1. "As I knew, or thought I knew, what was right or wrong, I did not see why I might not always do the one and avoid the other."

2. "While my care was employed in guarding against one fault, I was often surprised by another."

3. "I determined to give a week's strict attention to each of the virtues successively."

4. "I was surprised to find myself so much fuller of faults than I imagined."

5. "The man came every now and then from the wheel to see how the work went on, and at length would take his ax as it was, without further grinding. 'No,' said the smith, 'turn on, turn on; we shall have it bright by and by; as yet, it is only speckled.' 'Yes,' said the man, 'but I think I like a speckled ax best.'"

6. "... a perfect character might be attended with the inconvenience of being envied and hated; and that a benevolent man should allow a few faults in himself, to keep his friends in countenance."

Name _____ Date _____

from The Autobiography and from Poor Richard's Almanack by Benjamin Franklin
Reading Strategy: Draw Conclusions

Reading involves more than understanding the definition of each word in a sentence. The overall meaning may come from what an author *doesn't* tell you explicitly. To understand what an author is saying, **draw conclusions** based on supporting details and reasons in the text. For example, you may conclude that Benjamin Franklin does not like gossips, based on his value of the virtue of silence: "Speak not but what may benefit others or yourself; avoid trifling conversation."

Remember to draw conclusions based only on solid details and reasons. Unsupported conclusions may lead you away from the real meaning of a selection.

DIRECTIONS: *As you read the selections from Franklin's* The Autobiography *and* Poor Richard's Almanack, *identify several conclusions about Franklin, and record the supporting details and reasons in the following chart.*

Conclusion	Supporting Details and Reasons

Unit 2 Resources: A Nation Is Born

Name _____ Date _____

from **The Autobiography** and *from* **Poor Richard's Almanack** by Benjamin Franklin
Vocabulary Builder

Using the Root *-vigil*

A. DIRECTIONS: *The word root -vigil- can mean "remaining awake to watch or observe." The suffix -ance means "the state of"; -ant means "being in the state of." The prefix hyper- means "excessively; overly; too." Write a probable definition for each term.*

1. vigilant _____
2. hypervigilance _____

Using the Word List

arduous	avarice	fasting	vigilance
disposition	squander	felicity	foppery

B. DIRECTIONS: *Match each word on the left with its definition on the right. Write the letter of the definition in the blank next to the word it defines.*

___ 1. arduous
___ 2. avarice
___ 3. fasting
___ 4. disposition
___ 5. squander
___ 6. felicity
___ 7. vigilance
___ 8. foppery

A. happiness
B. watchfulness
C. difficult
D. waste
E. greed
F. foolish action
G. management
H. not eating

C. DIRECTIONS: *Circle the letter of the word that best completes each sentence.*

1. Her felicity was short-lived, however, and _____ once again reigned.
   A. joyousness B. sadness C. tidiness D. carelessness
2. His avarice was apparent, for he always _____ more money.
   A. lent B. borrowed C. wanted D. ignored
3. It was an arduous but _____ task.
   A. laborious B. strenuous C. exhausting D. rewarding
4. To squander each opportunity is to treat life as a _____.
   A. waste B. pleasure C. duty D. sign

Name _____ Date _____

from The Autobiography and from Poor Richard's Almanack by Benjamin Franklin
Grammar and Style: Pronoun Case

Pronoun case refers to the different forms a pronoun takes to show its function in a sentence. Use **subjective case pronouns** (such as *I, we, you, he, she, it,* and *they*) when the pronoun is the subject of the sentence or renames the subject after a linking verb. Use **objective case pronouns** (such as *me, us, you, him, her, it,* and *them*) when the pronoun receives the action of the verb or is the object of a preposition.

A. Practice: *These sentences are adapted from* The Autobiography. *Underline the subjective case pronouns and circle the objective case pronouns.*

1. The smith ground it bright for him.
2. In exchange, he only had to turn the wheel.
3. He turned, while the smith pressed the broad face of the ax hard and heavily on the stone, which made the turning of it very fatiguing.
4. "We shall have it bright by and by," said the smith.
5. "I like it best speckled," the man replied.

B. Writing Application: *Complete each sentence by writing the correct pronoun on the line.*

1. My classmates and _____ (I, me) read about Ben Franklin's list of virtues.
2. His attempts to better himself impressed my friend Jim and _____ (I, me).
3. Some other students and _____ (we, us) are investigating further.
4. Jim and _____ (they, them) are reading more of Franklin's autobiography.
5. Janis and _____ (he, him) are reading portions of *Poor Richard's Almanack*.
6. Jim and _____ (she, her) are also trying to follow Franklin's example.
7. For Janis and _____ (he, him), living up to Franklin's list of virtues may prove a difficult task.
8. The rest of the class is keeping an eye on Jim and _____ (she, her).
9. Even though Franklin lived centuries ago, his advice strikes the others and _____ (I, me) as very relevant to modern life.
10. In fact, the wisest founding father could have been _____ (he, him).

Name _____ Date _____

from The Autobiography and from Poor Richard's Almanack by Benjamin Franklin
Support for Writing

To prepare to write an **autobiographical account,** enter important information about an important experience in your life in the graphic organizer below. Choose an event that is memorable because you learned something from it.

Experience: Basic information When, Where	Others who had experience with me

Feelings I have about the experience	What I learned from the experience

On a separate page, use the information in your graphic organizer to write a draft of your autobiographical account. When you revise your draft, be sure to use transition words to make cause and effect relationships clear.

Unit 2 Resources: A Nation Is Born

Name _____ Date _____

from **The Autobiography** and *from* **Poor Richard's Almanack** by Benjamin Franklin
Support for Extend Your Learning

Listening and Speaking

Remembering Benjamin Franklin's wish to improve himself, work with a small group to have a brief class discussion about ways in which your class could improve. Use these ideas to formulate a **class improvement plan:** How will you define the steps to be taken? How will you record your efforts? What will your time frame be?

Present your group's plan to the rest of the class as an oral report. Ask for comments on the workability of your plan. Listen to other group plans.

Research and Technology

Work with a group to create a **travel brochure** for tourists who visit Philadelphia, Benjamin Franklin's long-time home. Use the Internet to gather information and download graphics. Enter information into the graphic organizer.

Philadelphia: Sites Related to Benjamin Franklin	Philadelphia: Art Museums, Restaurants, Parks
Philadelphia: Other American History Sites	Philadelphia: Hotels, Motels, Campgrounds

Create your travel brochure using a desktop publishing program. Place the finished product in your classroom library.

Name _____ Date _____

from **The Autobiography** and *from* **Poor Richard's Almanack** by Benjamin Franklin

Enrichment: Multiple Careers

A. DIRECTIONS: *Each career in the following table was held at one time by Benjamin Franklin. Decide which of Franklin's thirteen virtues could help a person succeed in each career. Write the virtues under each career.*

Writer	Printer	Inventor	Scientist	Politician	Diplomat

B. DIRECTIONS: *Choose one of the six careers. On the lines, summarize the virtues that apply to that career and the additional skills and abilities a person today would need to succeed in that career.*

Career: _____

_____

_____

_____

_____

_____

_____

_____

_____

_____

_____

_____

_____

_____

Name _____ Date _____

from The Autobiography and from Poor Richard's Almanack by Benjamin Franklin
Selection Test A

Critical Reading *Identify the letter of the choice that best answers the question.*

____ 1. Which part of this sentence from *The Autobiography* identifies it as an autobiography?

   I wished to live without committing any fault at any time.

   A. the word *I*
   B. the word *wished*
   C. the word *live*
   D. the word *time*

____ 2. Why is the selection by Franklin identified as an autobiography?
   A. Franklin is now dead.
   B. Franklin is famous.
   C. Franklin wrote about his own life.
   D. Franklin was a scientist.

____ 3. According to *The Autobiography*, what is Franklin's first step in his plan to reach perfection?
   A. He makes a list of what he wants to achieve.
   B. He improves his handwriting.
   C. He makes a schedule of what he does each day.
   D. He lists the friends he can count on.

____ 4. In *The Autobiography*, what does Franklin say keeps him from becoming a better person?
   A. his wish for money
   B. his need for power
   C. his own bad habits
   D. his choice of friends

____ 5. What conclusion can you draw about why Franklin has trouble staying organized, according to *The Autobiography*?
   A. He has very few responsibilities.
   B. He is always busy traveling.
   C. He likes to do things all at once.
   D. He has too many responsibilities.

___ 6. In *The Autobiography,* why does Franklin assign a week to each of the virtues he is trying to achieve?
   A. He has a limited amount of time to concentrate on his plan.
   B. He hopes the strength he gains each week will spill over into the next.
   C. He does not think that he can focus on more than one virtue at a time.
   D. He likes starting tasks on Monday and completing them on Sunday.

___ 7. In *The Autobiography,* Franklin believes that he can become a better person. What does this belief tell you about how he sees himself?
   A. He does not believe in himself.
   B. He has high hopes for himself.
   C. His knowledge of science can help him.
   D. His religion will help him.

___ 8. What information does *The Autobiography* reveal to readers about Franklin?
   A. his inventions
   B. important dates in his life
   C. what type of person he was
   D. what kind of family he came from

___ 9. Franklin writes in *The Autobiography* that even though he is old, he has not reached perfection. What conclusion can you draw from this information?
   A. He thinks it is still worthwhile to try to become a better person.
   B. He thinks he should just accept who he is.
   C. He thinks he should improve his handwriting.
   D. He thinks he should leave money to his children.

___ 10. Which reminder from *Poor Richard's Almanack* connects best to Franklin's ideas about trying to become a better person?
   A. "Three may keep a secret if two of them are dead."
   B. "'Tis easier to prevent bad habits than to break them."
   C. "If your head is wax, don't walk in the sun."
   D. "Keep thy shop, and they shop will keep thee."

___ 11. What is the best meaning of this aphorism from *Poor Richard's Almanack*?
   For want of a nail the shoe is lost; for want of a shoe the horse is lost; for want of a horse the rider is lost.
   A. Be sure to replace your lost tools and supplies.
   B. Small details can affect all of your work.
   C. Every rider should know how to shoe his horse.
   D. Horses run best when they do not have shoes.

Vocabulary and Grammar

____ 12. In which sentence is the meaning of the word *arduous* suggested?
   A. I have figured out how to do this task.
   B. I took one class each year.
   C. The task was very difficult for me.
   D. I used a ruler to set up my notes.

____ 13. Which of these passages contains a subjective case pronoun?
   A. I decided to use more information.
   B. His health was a gift to him.
   C. Her memory was not as sharp as his.
   D. Her children will follow her example.

Essay

14. Benjamin Franklin writes about his attempts to become a better person in *The Autobiography*. Think about his ideas about being organized; speaking only when it helps others; trying not to waste time or money; or being sincere. Which quality might make you a better person? In a brief essay, discuss a quality in yourself that you would like to improve.

15. *Poor Richard's Almanack* says to "Be slow in choosing a friend, slower in changing." What do you think this statement means? Write a brief essay, stating your ideas.

Name _____ Date _____

from The Autobiography and from Poor Richard's Almanack by Benjamin Franklin
Selection Test B

Critical Reading *Identify the letter of the choice that best completes the statement or answers the question.*

____ 1. How does Franklin begin his project to achieve moral perfection?
   A. He imitates engraved copies.
   B. He buys a speckled ax.
   C. He compiles thirteen virtues.
   D. He avoids trifling conversation.

____ 2. Which virtue is most difficult for Franklin to master?
   A. industry
   B. order
   C. sincerity
   D. temperance

____ 3. When Franklin first devised his project to attain moral perfection, he thought it would be difficult but possible to become perfect. What quality does this suggest that Franklin possessed?
   A. self-confidence
   B. pessimism
   C. sincerity
   D. common sense

____ 4. The list of virtues that Franklin draws up suggests that he was
   A. distracted and preoccupied.
   B. logical and orderly.
   C. impulsive and unpredictable.
   D. cynical and mistrustful.

____ 5. Which of these sentences most likely came from an autobiography?
   A. "I hope, therefore, that some of my descendants may follow the example and reap the benefit."
   B. "Philadelphia was a city at the heart of America's independence."
   C. "Benjamin Franklin also contributed to public service."
   D. "Almost everyone secretly desires to attain perfection in some field."

____ 6. In comparison to other books about Franklin, *The Autobiography* probably gives you the best insight into
   A. the moral values of the time.
   B. Franklin's inventions.
   C. Franklin's descendants.
   D. Franklin's personality.

____ 7. This work is classified as an autobiography because Franklin is
   A. a famous person.
   B. a famous person who is no longer living.
   C. the subject of the work.
   D. the subject and author of the work.

Name _____ Date _____

____ 8. Which of the following statements expresses an opinion?
   A. Franklin wrote an autobiography.
   B. Franklin was a great American.
   C. Franklin writes that he tried to live his life using thirteen virtues.
   D. Franklin admits that he never completely achieved perfection.

____ 9. Which passage needs the most interpretation in order to understand the author's meaning?
   A. "Different writers included more or fewer ideas under the same name."
   B. "I made a little book, in which I allotted a page for each of the virtues."
   C. "A benevolent man should allow a few faults in himself, to keep his friends in countenance."
   D. "I hope, therefore, that some of my descendants may follow the example and reap the benefit."

____ 10. Which of the following details gives the most information about the times in which Franklin lived?
   A. Franklin's desire for perfection
   B. the story of the speckled ax
   C. the references to Socrates and Pythagoras
   D. Franklin's desire to help his descendants

____ 11. What view of human nature is suggested by Franklin's aphorism "Three may keep a secret if two of them are dead"?
   A. Human beings like to gossip.
   B. People are naturally evil.
   C. All people are trustworthy.
   D. The secrets of the dead are impossible to discover.

____ 12. "Early to bed, early to rise, makes a man healthy, wealthy, and wise" is most closely related to which of these other aphorisms?
   A. "Fools make feasts, and wise men eat them."
   B. "If your head is wax, don't walk in the sun."
   C. "Dost thou love life? Then do not squander time; for that's the stuff life is made of."
   D. "Keep thy shop, and thy shop will keep thee."

Vocabulary and Grammar

____ 13. When Franklin called his project *arduous*, he meant it would be
   A. very difficult to do.
   B. easily done.
   C. very expensive.
   D. best done by a group.

____ 14. When Franklin spoke of the *felicity* of his life, he referred to
   A. outrageous events.
   B. frustrated feelings.
   C. happy times.
   D. fatiguing work.

___ 15. Identify the objective case pronoun in this passage: "Order, too, with regard to places for things, papers, etc., I found extremely difficult to acquire. I had not been early accustomed to it."
   A. the first *I*
   B. the second *I*
   C. *it*
   D. *too*

___ 16. Which of these statements contains an objective pronoun?
   A. What good shall I do this day?
   B. Contrary habits must be broken, and good ones acquired.
   C. They never reached the excellence of those copies.
   D. Like him, we all have a garden to weed.

Essay

17. *The Autobiography* was written by Franklin himself. Imagine you have read an account of Franklin's attempt to attain perfection written by an impartial reporter. Write an essay that compares and contrasts the versions written by Franklin and the reporter. Consider how each version would use facts and opinions.

18. Near the end of the selection, Franklin writes that a perfect character might be envied and hated. Write an essay in which you either support or reject this statement. Give reasons for your opinion. Support your position by drawing on the experiences Franklin had as he tried to attain the thirteen virtues.

19. Some people consider leisure time important to a person's good health, both mental and physical. The aphorism "Dost thou love life? Then do not squander time, for that's the stuff life is made of" seems to conflict with that view. Write an essay agreeing or disagreeing with the aphorism. Your essay should take into account your interpretation of the aphorism as well as the value you place on leisure time.

Name _____ Date _____

From the Scholar's Desk
William L. Andrews Introduces *The Interesting Narrative of the Life of Olaudah Equiano* by Olaudah Equiano

DIRECTIONS: *Use the space provided to answer the questions.*

1. At the beginning of his commentary, what surprising fact does the writer single out about the Middle Passage? How does this fact enhance the importance of Olaudah Equiano's narrative?
   _____
   _____
   _____
   _____

2. According to Andrews, why must it have been difficult for Equiano to compose his narrative?
   _____
   _____

3. What is the first stop on Equiano's "virtual tour" of the slave ship? What details does Equiano use to describe the scene on the ship's deck?
   _____
   _____
   _____

4. According to Andrews, with whom do readers of Equiano's narrative sympathize? From whom are readers alienated?
   _____
   _____

5. What does Andrews claim is the significance of Equiano's peek through the ship's quadrant? Does this claim sound justified, in your opinion? Briefly explain your answer.
   _____
   _____
   _____
   _____
   _____
   _____

Name _____ Date _____

William L. Andrews
Listening and Viewing

Segment 1: Meet William L. Andrews
- How did William L. Andrews first become interested in studying African American history and culture?
- How does Andrews act as a middle man between today's readers and nineteenth-century writers?

_____
_____
_____
_____

Segment 2: William L. Andrews Introduces Olaudah Equiano
- Why is Olaudah Equiano an important historical figure?
- What are slave narratives, and why do you think they are important to society?

_____
_____
_____
_____

Segment 3: The Writing Process
- Why does William L. Andrews want to know what primary sources say about the people he writes about?
- How would this information be helpful when reading a slave narrative?

_____
_____
_____
_____

Segment 4: The Rewards of Writing
- How can reading slave narratives have relevance to your life?
- What can today's reader learn by reading autobiographies such as Equiano's?

_____
_____
_____
_____

from The Interesting Narrative of the Life of Olaudah Equiano by Olaudah Equiano
Vocabulary Warm-up Word Lists

Study these words from the selection. Then, complete the activities.

Word List A

climate [KLY met] *n.* weather conditions of a particular region
　The lakeshore climate is very humid in the summertime.

confined [kun FYND] *v.* kept shut in; restricted
　The cats are confined to non-carpeted parts of the house.

dejected [dee JEK ted] *adj.* depressed; in low spirits
　The cocker spaniel gave us a dejected look when we left for the day.

intolerably [in TOL er eb lee] *adv.* unacceptably
　The music was intolerably loud, and some people wore earplugs.

persuaded [per SWAY ded] *v.* convinced
　Lisa persuaded her brother to give her five dollars.

render [REN der] *v.* make; provide
　The nursing staff will render assistance after your operation.

suffocated [SUF uh kay ted] *v.* stopped breathing
　Clouds of smoke nearly suffocated the puppy.

unmercifully [un MER si ful lee] *adv.* without pity
　The tennis star served unmercifully throughout the match.

Word List B

aggravated [AGG ruh vay ted] *v.* made worse or more troubling; irritated
　Helen was already late, so the traffic this morning really aggravated her.

avarice [AV uh riss] *n.* greed for riches
　Avarice, or greed, is one of the Seven Deadly Sins.

copious [KOH pee us] *adj.* plentiful; abundant
　We were impressed by the copious food at the banquet.

custody [KUS te dee] *n.* supervision; control; guard
　While in Grandma's custody, the children are not allowed to eat sweets.

gratify [GRAT uh fy] *v.* to please or satisfy
　Getting good grades will gratify your mother and father.

inseparable [in SEP uh re bl] *adj.* impossible to separate
　Mark and his best friend were inseparable throughout high school.

pacify [PASS uh fy] *v.* calm; soothe
　Quiet music will often pacify the baby.

undergo [un der GOH] *v.* endure or suffer; experience
　Gymnasts undergo very difficult training.

Name _____   Date _____

from The Interesting Narrative of the Life of Olaudah Equiano by Olaudah Equiano
Vocabulary Warm-up Exercises

Exercise A *Fill in the blanks, using each word from Word List A. Use each word only once.*

In our part of the country, the [1] _____ is usually very hot in the summer, and this week has been a real scorcher. Yesterday it was [2] _____ hot and stuffy in our apartment. We were all feeling cooped up and uncomfortable because we were [3] _____ to a few small rooms. We were getting pretty glum and [4] _____, so we [5] _____ my mom to take us to the beach. At the shore, the sand was hot and the sun beat down [6] _____, but the waves were cool and the breeze was wonderful. At the end of the day, we did have to go back to our apartment and be almost [7] _____ again. But I'm sure of one thing. A trip to the beach can at least [8] _____ the summer heat tolerable for a little while.

Exercise B *Decide whether each statement below is true or false. Circle T or F, and explain your answer.*

1. If you are given <u>copious</u> amounts of work, you do not have much to do.
   T / F _____

2. If your condition is <u>aggravated</u>, you are feeling better and better.
   T / F _____

3. If a boy and his dog are <u>inseparable</u>, they are always together.
   T / F _____

4. If you decide to <u>undergo</u> medical treatment, you refuse to let a doctor take care of you.
   T / F _____

5. If a pet is left in your <u>custody</u>, you have the responsibility to watch over it.
   T / F _____

6. If a government wants to <u>pacify</u> its critics, it wants to fight and destroy them.
   T / F _____

7. If you <u>gratify</u> your desire for power, you gain the power you want.
   T / F _____

8. If you are known for your <u>avarice</u>, people respect you for your generosity.
   T / F _____

Unit 2 Resources: A Nation Is Born
© Pearson Education, Inc., publishing as Pearson Prentice Hall. All rights reserved.

Name _____ Date _____

from The Interesting Narrative of the Life of Olaudah Equiano by Olaudah Equiano
Reading Warm-up A

Read the following passage. Pay special attention to the underlined words. Then, read it again, and complete the activities. Use a separate sheet of paper for your written answers.

A remarkable art exhibit of unique paintings by John W. Jones opened recently in Charleston, North Carolina. What makes the paintings unique is that they are based on old engravings of scenes of slavery. Jones discovered these scenes printed on the paper money of the Confederate States of America. Jones made his discovery in 1996 when someone gave him a Confederate ten-dollar bill showing a black field hand at work. The artist realized that most people were not aware that African Americans were pictured on money.

Jones began to collect similar bills, and he has since created over 90 colorful canvases based on them. In the engravings, slaves are not shown as being <u>intolerably</u> treated or working in unacceptably harsh conditions. This is because the images were a form of propaganda, promoting the moneymaking values of slavery. Slaves are shown clearing farmland, planting and carrying cotton, harvesting corn and tobacco. They are shown taking care of horses, working in factories, and even working on a wheat farm for George Washington. The slaves are depicted as hard-working and even happy, not <u>dejected</u> and depressed.

The slaves on the bills are portrayed as well-treated, not <u>unmercifully</u> overworked, because one of the purposes of the engravings was to promote slavery as a vital economic force in a thriving economy. The slaves are shown working in flourishing landscapes of the hot Southern <u>climate</u>. They are not <u>confined</u> in small rooms or <u>suffocated</u> in close quarters. Jones's paintings bring these vignettes to life, transforming propaganda into art.

Jones's paintings have drawn crowds to museums. The artist hopes his work will make people more aware of the past and <u>render</u> the African American experience even more central to the history of the American economy. <u>Persuaded</u> by the power of the imagery, some schools now use the paintings as a curriculum resource.

1. Circle the word that means the same as <u>intolerably</u>. Describe an *intolerably* irritating experience you have had.

2. Underline the word that means the same as <u>dejected</u>. Name something people do to avoid feeling *dejected*.

3. Circle the part of <u>unmercifully</u> that means "not." Use *unmercifully* in a sentence.

4. Circle the words that help explain <u>climate</u>. Describe the *climate* in your state.

5. Underline the words that help explain <u>confined</u>. Name two places in which someone can be *confined*.

6. Circle the words that help explain <u>suffocated</u>. Define *suffocated* in your own words.

7. Underline the word that means the same as <u>render</u>. Name one way you would *render* your school day a better one.

8. Circle the words that tell what some schools were <u>persuaded</u> to do. Describe a time an advertisement *persuaded* you to buy something.

from The Interesting Narrative of the Life of Olaudah Equiano by Olaudah Equiano
Reading Warm-up B

Read the following passage. Pay special attention to the underlined words. Then, read it again, and complete the activities. Use a separate sheet of paper for your written answers.

The Middle Passage is the name given to the transatlantic transportation of slaves to the New World, a horrific ordeal that African men, women, and children had to undergo on their way to a life of slavery in America. They had to endure great physical privation, aggravated by the mental anguish they also suffered; that is, their pain and hunger were made worse by fear and despair.

Ten to twelve million Africans were sold into slavery from the fifteenth through the nineteenth centuries. They were the victims of two widespread and corrupt forces—racism that made slavery morally and socially acceptable, and avarice, the greed for profit no matter what the products bought and sold. To gratify their desire for riches, Europeans built trading posts along the coast of Africa where they traded cloth, guns, and other items for human beings.

African husbands and wives, parents and children, brothers and sisters, who had thought they would remain inseparable their whole lives, were torn apart. Those who survived the forced march from the continental interior were loaded onto ships and experienced copious suffering, the many unspeakable aspects of being reduced to property. Ultimately, the survivors were released from the custody of the ship captains who were in charge of them and sold at auction.

One small way in which Africans who were left behind attempted to pacify their feelings and soothe their profound sense of loss was to compose songs of lamentation about those kidnapped into slavery. A Kwa chant mourns the disappearance of an eleven-year-old boy taken in 1755, Olaudah Equiano: *Who are we looking for, who are we looking for? / It's Equiano we're looking for. / Has he gone to the stream? Let him come back. / Has he gone to the farm? Let him return. / It's Equiano we're looking for.*

1. Underline the word that means the same as undergo. Describe an experience you once had to *undergo*.

2. Circle the words that mean the same as aggravated. Name two antonyms of *aggravated*.

3. Underline the word that means the same as avarice. Use *avarice* in a sentence.

4. Circle the words that tell what people wanted to gratify. Define *gratify* in your own words.

5. Underline the words that help explain inseparable by meaning its opposite. Name two things that are often considered *inseparable*.

6. Circle the word that means about the same as copious. Describe a landscape in which something is *copious*.

7. Circle the words that explain custody. Use *custody* in a sentence about babysitting.

8. Underline the word that means the same as pacify. Name something a salesperson can do to *pacify* an angry customer.

Unit 2 Resources: A Nation Is Born

Name _____   Date _____

from *The Interesting Narrative of the Life of Olaudah Equiano* by Olaudah Equiano
Literary Analysis: Slave Narratives

A **slave narrative** is an autobiographical account of life as a slave. Often written to expose the horrors of human bondage, it documents a slave's experiences from his or her own point of view. The selection from Equiano's narrative provides an especially grim description of the long voyage from Africa to Barbados that Equiano was forced to endure when he was only eleven years old.

Among the indignities that Equiano put up with while a slave was the unwelcomed changing of his name. During his lifetime, Equiano was known by three different names. His African name was Olaudah Equiano. His American master from Virginia decided to change Equiano's name to Jacob. A short time later, an English merchant purchased "Jacob," took him to England, and renamed him again.

DIRECTIONS: *Read the following excerpt from Equiano's autobiography. Then answer the questions on the lines provided.*

> Some of the people of the ship used to tell me they were going to carry me back to my own country and this made me very happy. I was quite rejoiced at the sound of going back, and thought if I should get home what wonders I should have to tell. But I was reserved for another fate and was soon undeceived when we come within sight of the English coast. While I was on board this ship, my captain and master named me Gustavus Vassa. I at that time began to understand him a little, and refused to be called so, and told him as well as I could that I would be called Jacob; but he said I should not, and still called me Gustavus; and when I refused to answer to my new name, which at first I did, it gained me many a cuff; so at length I submitted and was obliged to bear the present name, by which I have been known ever since.

1. Slave narratives contain vivid accounts of oppression. What examples of oppression appear in the passage above? _____
   _____

2. In what way was Equiano's response to the change in his name different from his response to the oppression he suffered on his voyage from Africa? How do you account for the difference?
   _____
   _____

3. Why might Equiano have asked the captain to call him Jacob rather than Olaudah?
   _____
   _____

4. Look up Gustavus I in an encyclopedia. Then write who Equiano was named after. Was this name an appropriate choice? Why? _____
   _____

Name _____ Date _____

from **The Interesting Narrative of the Life of Olaudah Equiano** by Olaudah Equiano
Reading Strategy: Summarizing

When you **summarize** a passage or a selection, you state briefly in your own words its main ideas and most important details. A good way of checking your understanding of a text, summarizing is especially helpful when you read material written in another time period or in an unfamiliar style.

A. DIRECTIONS: *As you read or reread the selection by Olaudah Equiano, fill out this chart to help you keep track of the main ideas and key details you need to include in your summary. One sample entry has been done for you.*

Main Ideas	Details
The slaves on the ship were kept in close confinement under terrible conditions.	terrible stench; crowded; filthy; shrieks and groans; many perish; Equiano thinks death would be a relief

B. DIRECTIONS: *Use the chart you completed to write a summary of the selection on the lines provided.*

_____
_____
_____
_____
_____
_____
_____

Name _____   Date _____

from **The Interesting Narrative of the Life of Olaudah Equiano** by Olaudah Equiano
Vocabulary Builder

Using the Root *-vid-*

A. DIRECTIONS: *The word root -vid-, from the Latin* videre, *means "to see." On the lines provided, explain how each word that follows conveys the meaning of the root.*

1. videotape _____

2. evident _____

Using the Word List

| loathsome | copious | pacify |
| pestilential | improvident | avarice |

B. DIRECTIONS: *On the line, write the letter of the definition before the word it defines.*

___ 1. copious   A. disgusting; offensive
___ 2. avarice   B. abundant
___ 3. pacify   C. greed
___ 4. pestilential   D. lacking thrift or foresight
___ 5. improvident   E. to make peaceful
___ 6. loathsome   F. causing infection

C. DIRECTIONS: *On the line provided, write the word from the Word List that best completes each sentence. Use each word only once.*

1. Smith's sin was _____, for he pursued wealth with single-minded devotion.

2. The old sailors told horror tales of a _____ sea monster.

3. Given their lack of resources, making a long journey seemed _____.

4. The newcomers fell ill, the strange climate proving _____ to them.

5. They hoped their gifts would _____ any hostile natives they encountered.

6. The island was lush, with _____ natural resources.

Name _____ Date _____

from **The Interesting Narrative of the Life of Olaudah Equiano** by Olaudah Equiano
Grammar and Style: Active and Passive Voice

A verb is in the **active voice** when the subject of the sentence or clause performs the action. A verb is in the **passive voice** when the action is performed on the subject. The passive voice consists of a form of the helping verb *be* plus the past participle of the main verb.

Active Voice: I *expected* every hour to share the fate of my companions.

Passive Voice: We *were conducted* immediately to the merchant's yard.

The passive voice is suitable when the performer of the action is unknown, unimportant, or best concealed. Otherwise, use the active voice to make your writing more forceful and effective.

A. Practice: *On the line before each number, write* A *if the verb is in the active voice and* P *if it is in the passive voice. Then, on the long line provided, rewrite the sentence using a verb in the opposite voice, adding or dropping words as necessary.*

____ 1. The ship took in all the cargo.
_____

____ 2. The groans of the dying turned the scene into almost inconceivable horror.
_____

____ 3. Two of the wretches were drowned.
_____

B. Writing Application: *In the following sentences based on the selection by Equiano, the verbs are all in the passive voice. Decide if each would be more effective in the active voice. If so, rewrite the sentence on the lines provided, adding or dropping words as necessary. If not, explain your reasons for leaving the verb in the passive voice.*

1. Equiano and his sister were kidnapped from their home in West Africa.
_____
_____

2. During the journey across the ocean, Equiano was separated from his sister.
_____
_____

3. At the merchant's in Barbados, the captives were confined to a yard.
_____
_____

Name _____ Date _____

from **The Interesting Narrative of the Life of Olaudah Equiano** by Olaudah Equiano
Support for Writing

To create your **museum exhibit placard,** use the Internet to do research on the slave trade. Create a time line to document the major steps in the life of a captured slave, from capture to slave auction. Also use information from the selection by Olaudah Equiano.

The Slave Trade: A Time Line

Level 1

Capture _____

Boarding Slave Ship: Physical Set-Up of Ship _____

Early Events During Journey _____

Level 2

Later Events: How Slaves Resisted _____

Landing in New World _____

Sale of Slaves at Auction _____

Check to see that the placard has all of the information you have collected. Make sure the time sequence is clear and that the format is graphically pleasing.

Name _____ Date _____

from The Interesting Narrative of the Life of Olaudah Equiano by Olaudah Equiano
Support for Extend Your Learning

Listening and Speaking

Before you present your **debate** on whether slavery can exist in today's societies, use these tips:

- Create "pro" and "con" teams.
- Develop key arguments.
- Find supporting evidence.
- Assign positions for introductory arguments, rebuttals, and conclusions.

Stage the debate for the class, and respond to questions from your audience.

Research and Technology

Prepare a **research presentation** on the organization Amnesty International. Use the Internet or the library to research the causes it publicizes and some of the prisoners it has helped to get released. Enter your information in the graphic organizer below.

Amnesty International

Level 1

Amnesty International: Where It Operates	Mission of Organization

Level 2

List of Injustices	Example of A Campaign

Level 3

Example of A Political Prisoner	Results of Campaign to Free Him/Her

Present your findings to the class. Ask for critical responses and questions.

Name _____   Date _____

from **The Interesting Narrative of the Life of Olaudah Equiano** by Olaudah Equiano
Enrichment: Film Portrayals of the Slave Trade

The great value of Olaudah Equiano's first-hand account of life aboard a slave ship lies in his ability to personalize the slavery experience. We shrink in horror at his descriptions of brutal floggings, loathsome smells, and anguished screams of women and children because Equiano has put us on that ship. As we read, *we* are a slave—captured, imprisoned, terrified of our future, desperate to survive. We recoil at the depravity and marvel at the strength of the human spirit.

Has Hollywood done as well in shaping our view of the slave trade in America? After all, most of us have formed our impressions of slavery, not from first-hand accounts such as Equiano's, but from films and television movies. Do these films show Hollywood stereotypes or do they present what you consider to be true-to-life depictions?

A. DIRECTIONS: *View a film or portion of a film that depicts some aspect of the slave trade, such as* Amistad *or the early episodes of the television series* Roots. *You may borrow these or similar films from your local library or video store. After you have viewed the films, compare and contrast them with the selection. Focus on the historical accuracy of the film as it compares to Olaudah Equiano's narrative. Write your analysis on the lines provided.*

_____
_____
_____
_____
_____
_____
_____
_____
_____
_____
_____
_____
_____
_____
_____
_____

Name _____ Date _____

from **The Interesting Narrative of the Life of Olaudah Equiano** by Olaudah Equiano
Selection Test A

Critical Reading *Identify the letter of the choice that best answers the question.*

___ 1. What does Equiano describe in *The Interesting Narrative of the Life of Olaudah Equiano?*
  A. the loss of his African culture
  B. the ocean journey on a slave ship
  C. the struggle to abolish slavery
  D. the sea life he observed on board

___ 2. How does *The Interesting Narrative of the Life of Olaudah Equiano* describe slavery?
  A. with anger
  B. with confusion
  C. with acceptance
  D. with humor

___ 3. In *The Interesting Narrative of the Life of Olaudah Equiano*, Equiano mentions "many of the inhabitants of the deep" who were happier than he was. Who or what is he describing?
  A. the slaves asleep in the ship's hold
  B. the slaves who jumped into the sea
  C. the fish and other ocean creatures
  D. the slave traders asleep in their cabins

___ 4. Why did Olaudah Equiano write *The Interesting Narrative of the Life of Olaudah Equiano?*
  A. to contrast life in Africa and Barbados
  B. to entertain readers with sea stories
  C. to persuade readers of slavery's evil
  D. to inform readers about marine life

___ 5. Which detail would probably be left out of a summary of *The Interesting Narrative of the Life of Olaudah Equiano?*
  A. The crew ate the fish they caught.
  B. Most slaves were kept in the ship's hold.
  C. The ship's conditions were terrible.
  D. Many slaves were infected with disease.

Unit 2 Resources: A Nation Is Born
© Pearson Education, Inc., publishing as Pearson Prentice Hall. All rights reserved.

Name _____ Date _____

_____ 6. Which is the best summary of *The Interesting Narrative of the Life of Olaudah Equiano*?
A. The journey went from Africa to North America.
B. The ocean crossings were horrible for slaves.
C. Equiano escaped being chained because he was ill.
D. The air on slave ships was filthy.

_____ 7. What gives *The Interesting Narrative of the Life of Olaudah Equiano* its strength?
A. its poetic words and figures of speech
B. its similarity to an African folk tale
C. its power as a personal account
D. its logical arguments against slavery

_____ 8. "Necessary tubs" were used for people's basic needs in *The Interesting Narrative of the Life of Olaudah Equiano*. What were they?
A. tubs of fish
B. lifeboats
C. food containers
D. toilets

_____ 9. In *The Interesting Narrative of the Life of Olaudah Equiano*, why did slaves jump off the ship?
A. They preferred death to slavery.
B. They hoped to swim to shore.
C. They wanted to give others more room.
D. They hoped to find another boat.

_____ 10. In *The Interesting Narrative of the Life of Olaudah Equiano*, why didn't the slaves want to leave the ship in Barbados?
A. They were afraid they would be eaten.
B. They were afraid they would get lost.
C. They were afraid they would be sent home.
D. They were afraid they would not know anyone.

_____ 11. If you were summarizing the end of *The Interesting Narrative of the Life of Olaudah Equiano*, which of the following would you use as the main idea?
A. The traders shouted with joy when they reached Barbados.
B. Old slaves reassured the new captives.
C. The Africans in Barbados spoke many languages.
D. When the ship landed, the slaves were sold to buyers.

___ 12. In *The Interesting Narrative of the Life of Olaudah Equiano,* what does Equiano remember that helped him learn more about how sailors travel?
   A. listening to a drum signal the slaves' sale
   B. looking through the quadrant to find land
   C. being put into the merchant's yard
   D. seeing ships in the Barbados harbor

___ 13. Why did the crew stop the slaves from jumping overboard in *The Interesting Narrative of the Life of Olaudah Equiano?*
   A. They didn't want the slaves to escape.
   B. They didn't want to end the voyage.
   C. They didn't want the slaves to swim.
   D. They didn't want the captain to get angry.

Vocabulary and Grammar

___ 14. In which sentence is the meaning of the word *avarice* suggested?
   A. The dreadful air caused illness.
   B. Slave buyers wanted to make money.
   C. The slaves wanted the extra fish.
   D. Many planters came to Barbados.

___ 15. Which of the following sentences contains a verb in the passive voice?
   A. One day they took a number of fishes.
   B. Two of the wretches were drowned.
   C. The whites on board gave a great shout.
   D. We did not know what to think of this.

Essay

16. Why do you think the slave traders filled their ships with so many Africans? They must have known that there was too little room for so many people and that many would die. Write a brief essay that explains why they might have made this decision.

17. Consider the kinds of skills Olaudah Equiano must have had in order to write this narrative of his time on board the slave ship. Write a brief essay to discuss the skills he would have had to have or develop.

Name _____ Date _____

from The Interesting Narrative of the Life of Olaudah Equiano by Olaudah Equiano
Selection Test B

Critical Reading *Identify the letter of the choice that best completes the statement or answers the question.*

___ 1. What experience does this portion of Equiano's slave narrative describe?
   A. the loss of African cultural traditions
   B. the fight to abolish slavery
   C. the observations of a slave merchant
   D. the horrors slaves faced on transatlantic voyages

___ 2. What attitude toward slavery does the narrative most strongly convey?
   A. outrage
   B. understanding
   C. tolerance
   D. indifference

___ 3. Why does Equiano feel that the hardships, some of which he cannot even bear to relate, are "inseparable" from the slave trade?
   A. Sailing in those days meant perilous hardships for all who sailed.
   B. Because captives will always resist bondage, slave traders will always institute harsh measures to control the slaves.
   C. The slave traders know only harsh measures and no other way.
   D. Because slavery is a form of commercial enterprise, those who engage in it are invariably greedy and cruel.

___ 4. What was Equiano's main purpose in writing *The Interesting Narrative*?
   A. to entertain readers with dramatic episodes in his life
   B. to sway public opinion about slavery
   C. to contrast life in Africa and life in Barbados
   D. to provide detailed information on 18th-century sea travel

___ 5. Much of the power of this selection stems from the fact that it is
   A. filled with highly poetic imagery and figures of speech.
   B. similar in style to an African folk tale.
   C. a logical, well-reasoned argument.
   D. a personal narrative.

___ 6. Which of these details expresses the most objective viewpoint?
   A. Equiano got seasick when he was on the ship.
   B. Looking through the quadrant made Equiano think the world was magic.
   C. The cries of slaves saddened Equiano.
   D. The flying fish amazed Equiano as they flew across the ship.

___ 7. The narrator was placed on the deck of the ship because
   A. there was no room for him below deck.
   B. he was being punished, and the wind and rain were fierce.
   C. his captors feared he might die below deck.
   D. conditions below deck were unpleasant.

Unit 2 Resources: A Nation Is Born
© Pearson Education, Inc., publishing as Pearson Prentice Hall. All rights reserved.

____ 8. What happens to the captives who try to get the extra fish the slave traders caught?
   A. They share the fish with the other captives.
   B. They devour the fish instantly.
   C. They are caught and flogged.
   D. They are allowed to cook and eat the fish for supper.

____ 9. Which detail most clearly shows that not every sailor on the slave ship was always cruel to the slaves?
   A. the crew's preventing additional suicides after some captives jump overboard
   B. the mariner's giving Equiano the quadrant to look through
   C. the sailors' tossing the extra fish back into the sea
   D. the sailors' treatment of those captives who tried to get the extra fish

____ 10. Which detail would probably not be important enough to include in a summary of the first paragraph of the selection?
   A. The crowded conditions made the ship unbearable.
   B. Most of the captives were kept below deck.
   C. The captives' chains chaffed their skin.
   D. Disease was rampant aboard the ship.

____ 11. Often did I think many of the inhabitants of the deep much more happy than myself. I envied them the freedom they enjoyed.

   In this passage, "inhabitants of the deep" refers to
   A. fish and other sea creatures.
   B. the slaves who were below deck.
   C. the slaves who had jumped overboard.
   D. the children who had fallen into the necessary tubs.

____ 12. If you were summarizing the selection, which statement would you use to express the main idea of the last section?
   A. The traders were overjoyed at reaching Barbados.
   B. The captives were afraid that they would be eaten.
   C. The ship landed, and the captives were sold into slavery.
   D. Old slaves joined the newcomers from Africa to tell them about their fate.

____ 13. Based on the interests Equiano shows in this selection, if freed from slavery, he would most likely become
   A. an abolitionist or a sailor.
   B. a merchant or a planter.
   C. a professor or an abolitionist.
   D. a slave owner or a slave trader.

Vocabulary and Grammar

____ 14. What is the meaning of the root *-vid-*?
   A. to die
   B. to hunt for
   C. to see
   D. to find

____ 15. Which word is closest in meaning to *copious*?
   A. scarce
   B. plentiful
   C. scattered
   D. duplicated

____ 16. Which word is most nearly opposite in meaning to *pacify*?
   A. enrage
   B. appease
   C. ignore
   D. subdue

____ 17. Which sentence below uses a verb in the passive voice?
   A. At last, we came in sight of the island of Barbados.
   B. We were conducted immediately to the merchant's yard.
   C. We were not many days in the merchant's custody.
   D. The buyers rush at once into the yard.

Essay

18. Imagine being enslaved under the harsh conditions described by Equiano. Write a version of the narrative from your own point of view. Based on the information in Equiano's narrative, summarize the shipboard conditions, and then express what you think would be your own reactions.

19. Slave narratives were valuable tools in abolitionists' hands. Based on the details in this selection, explain why Equiano's narrative would have been helpful in the fight to abolish slavery. Cite details from the selection and the effects you think they would have on readers. Also consider how abolitionists might have used some of the details in their arguments against slavery.

20. As the biographical sketch preceding the selection suggests, Olaudah Equiano was truly a remarkable man. Write an essay in which you describe his personality, attitudes, and skills and attributes based on clues in the selection. Cite his own remarks and other details, and then consider the conclusions you can draw about him.

The Declaration of Independence by Thomas Jefferson
from **The Crisis, Number 1** by Thomas Paine

Vocabulary Warm-up Word Lists

Study these words from the selections. Then, complete the activities.

Word List A

absolute [ab so LOOT] *adj.* perfect in quality or nature; complete
  With <u>absolute</u> confidence, Jennifer stepped upon the field.

burden [BUR den] *n.* something that is difficult to carry or endure
  Taking care of a younger sibling can sometimes be a <u>burden</u>.

entitle [en TY tel] *v.* give a right or claim to something
  This coupon will <u>entitle</u> you to a free ice cream cone.

impel [im PEL] *v.* force; urge; push
  These are the reasons that <u>impel</u> me to quit this job.

inevitably [in EV it uh blee] *adv.* in such a way that could not be otherwise
  The city spends a lot of money, so the fireworks will <u>inevitably</u> be good.

invariably [in VAIR ee uh blee] *adv.* in a constant, consistent manner
  Jim is forgetful, and he will <u>invariably</u> misplace his wallet.

pursuit [pur SOOT] *n.* the act of try to catch or attain something
  I hope that each of you will continue your <u>pursuit</u> of a good education.

rejoice [ree JOYSS] *v.* feel joyful; be delighted
  Hannah will <u>rejoice</u> when she hears of her sister's good fortune.

Word List B

abolish [uh BOL ish] *v.* do away with
  The Vermont Constitution was the first to <u>abolish</u> slavery.

compliance [kum PLY uhns] *n.* act of following requests or rules
  The infant car seat is made in <u>compliance</u> with safety regulations.

consolation [kon suh LAY shun] *n.* comfort
  Sad because of his team's loss, Alan needs <u>consolation</u> right now.

depriving [dee PRYV ing] *v.* taking away; keeping from having or using
  Your decision is <u>depriving</u> us of a great opportunity.

deriving [di RYV ing] *v.* obtaining or receiving from a source
  Bob is always <u>deriving</u> knowledge from reading and listening.

obstructing [ob STRUKT ing] *v.* blocking; preventing
  The man with the big hat was <u>obstructing</u> our view.

prudent [PROO dent] *adj.* wise in practical matters; using good judgment
  It is a wise person who is <u>prudent</u> with money.

tyranny [TEER uh nee] *n.* absolute power, especially when cruel or unjust
  In many countries, the fight against <u>tyranny</u> is not over.

Name _____ Date _____

The Declaration of Independence by Thomas Jefferson
from The Crisis, Number 1 by Thomas Paine
Vocabulary Warm-up Exercises

Exercise A *Fill in the blanks, using each word from Word List A. Use each word only once.*

This year, our soccer team is playing brilliantly and is in hot [1] _____ of the championship. In previous years, we played poorly [2] _____ giving up too many goals, and rarely scoring. [3] _____, we became the laughing stock of the league—but not this year. This season our goalie is an [4] _____ magician, making seemingly impossible saves. We now have the kind of team spirit that [5] _____ us to play our hearts out. Our main rivals have the skill and the confidence that seem to [6] _____ them to win it all, but we've beaten them once this year, and we can do it again. Losing year after year can be a heavy [7] _____, and we're all looking forward to lifting that weight off our shoulders. What a feeling it will be to [8] _____ at a championship celebration!

Exercise B *Answer the questions with complete explanations.*

1. If you are in <u>compliance</u> with all federal regulations, are you violating any of them?
   _____

2. If road workers are <u>obstructing</u> the street, is the street clear?
   _____

3. If you are <u>depriving</u> yourself of fatty foods, can you eat anything you want?
   _____

4. If you give a prize to someone who did not win first place, why is it called a <u>consolation</u> prize?
   _____

5. Is spending all your money at one time a <u>prudent</u> thing to do?
   _____

6. If you want to <u>abolish</u> a law, do you want to make sure that law lasts for a long time?
   _____

7. If you support <u>tyranny</u>, do you believe a ruler should be all-powerful?
   _____

8. If you are <u>deriving</u> great pleasure from a book, do you think the book is delightful?
   _____

The Declaration of Independence by Thomas Jefferson
from **The Crisis, Number 1** by Thomas Paine
Reading Warm-up A

Read the following passage. Pay special attention to the underlined words. Then, read it again, and complete the activities. Use a separate sheet of paper for your written answers.

When we think of colonial patriots, we <u>invariably</u> think of the Founding Fathers or Washington's army, almost always ignoring the lesser-known Sons of Liberty. In 1765, secret resistance groups around the country began to work together under the name "The Sons of Liberty." These American patriots played a vital role in organizing opposition to British injustice.

Most of the Sons of Liberty were middle-class or even upper-class Americans. The <u>pursuit</u> of violence, seeking the overthrow of the government, was not one of their principles. Their immediate goal was the repeal of the Stamp Act. They believed strongly that the law did not <u>entitle</u> the British to impose the tax. They believed that Parliament did not have the right to levy any tax that the colonial legislature did not approve.

The Sons used every means at their disposal to <u>impel</u> every American to oppose the Stamp Act. They urged complete and <u>absolute</u> resistance to what they considered the unreasonable and unjust tax <u>burden</u> laid on the shoulders of Americans. Such taxes were a financial and political weight they believed they should not have to bear.

The Sons of Liberty did work with more radical groups, and sometimes violence did erupt. In 1766, the Sons in New York disrupted a theater performance, drove the audience out into the street, pulled down the building, and turned it into a bonfire. Sam Adams and Paul Revere led the Sons in Massachusetts, and these patriots realized that they would <u>inevitably</u> have to resort to violence. They knew that conflict and even war could not be prevented.

The Sons were able to <u>rejoice</u> at the repeal of the Stamp Act in 1766, but their happiness and satisfaction soon disappeared. When the Townshend Acts were imposed by the British, the Sons became even more active and remained so until the Revolution.

1. Circle the words that help explain <u>invariably</u>. Name something that *invariably* happens to you.

2. Underline the word that explains <u>pursuit</u>. What do you think people mean by "the *pursuit* of happiness"?

3. Circle the words that explain <u>entitle</u>. Use *entitle* in a sentence.

4. Underline the word that means about the same as <u>impel</u>. What do you think should *impel* Americans to vote?

5. Circle the word that helps explain <u>absolute</u>. Name a song that you think is an *absolute* masterpiece.

6. Underline the words that help explain <u>burden</u>. Name something you consider a *burden*.

7. Circle the words that explain <u>inevitably</u>. Define *inevitably* in your own words.

8. Underline the words that explain <u>rejoice</u>. Name something that makes you *rejoice*.

The Declaration of Independence by Thomas Jefferson
from **The Crisis, Number 1** by Thomas Paine
Reading Warm-up B

Read the following passage. Pay special attention to the underlined words. Then, read it again, and complete the activities. Use a separate sheet of paper for your written answers.

The American Revolution so often seems to be an all-male drama, with modern Americans <u>deriving</u> their sense of it from books and movies about male patriots. In the twenty-first century, we should not obtain our ideas of the Revolution from such limited sources. A new book by historian Carol Berkin sets out to tell the story of the Revolution with a deeper and wider focus.

Revolutionary Mothers explores the roles of women during the war against British <u>tyranny</u>. It details the many ways women opposed the unjust and willful rule of England. Women, for example, were effective spies and saboteurs—careful and <u>prudent</u>, balancing bravery with good judgment. Women ran farms, plantations, and businesses when their husbands were away. Women even took part in combat. Berkin tells the story of Margaret Corbin, who was crippled for life when she valiantly took her husband's place manning a cannon at Fort Monmouth.

Women were the prime force in the boycotts that caused the British to <u>abolish</u> the hated tax laws. To force the British to do away with the laws, American female consumers enforced <u>compliance</u> with the boycotts. They persuaded people to go along with the refusal to buy taxed products. They knew that <u>obstructing</u> trade and preventing merchants from making profits would eventually bring about change. They felt confident that <u>depriving</u> themselves of things, not having or using some domestic items, even necessary ones, would gradually have a powerful effect.

Although American colonial histories are still dominated by men, it is some <u>consolation</u> to know that historians continue to unearth all that was accomplished by women during that period. Books like Professor Berkin's give some comfort to those who have always felt certain that the history of America is a complex tale that still needs more research.

1. Underline the word that explains *deriving*. Name the tools you use most often for *deriving* information.

2. Circle the words that define *tyranny*. What is the noun that names a person who engages in *tyranny*?

3. Underline the words that explain *prudent*. Use *prudent* in a sentence.

4. Circle the words that mean the same as *abolish*. Name a law, custom, or attitude that you would like to *abolish*.

5. Underline the words that help explain *compliance*. Use *compliance* in a sentence.

6. Circle the word that means about the same as *obstructing*. Describe a situation in which something is *obstructing* your progress.

7. Circle the words that explain *depriving*. Use *depriving* in a sentence about self-control.

8. Underline the word that means the same as *consolation*. Describe a situation in which you were able to provide someone with *consolation*.

Name _____   Date _____

The Declaration of Independence by Thomas Jefferson
from The Crisis, Number 1 by Thomas Paine
Literary Analysis: Persuasion

Persuasion is writing that attempts to convince readers to accept a specific viewpoint about an issue and to take a particular action. A good persuasive writer generally uses a combination of logical and emotional appeals, involving the audience both intellectually and emotionally in order to persuade them thoroughly.

A **logical appeal** uses a chain of reasoning to establish the validity of a proposed argument. Whether reasoning from particular examples to a general conclusion, or from the general to the specific, writers use evidence to persuade their audiences intellectually. Notice how Paine moves from specific evidence to more general remarks in the chain of reasoning he presents here.

> Britain, with an army to enforce her tyranny, has declared that she has a right (*not only to* TAX) but "*to* BIND *us* in ALL CASES WHATSOEVER," and if being *bound in that manner,* is not slavery, then is there not such a thing as slavery upon earth.

An **emotional appeal** seeks to stir the reader's feelings. It relies not so much on reasoned arguments as on charged words and symbols that evoke sympathy or distaste. Among the strongest emotional appeals are anecdotes or examples that dramatize a situation. For instance, Paine's story of the Tory tavernkeeper and his nine-year-old child makes a strong appeal to the human desire to ensure a good future for one's children.

A. DIRECTIONS: *For each of these passages, clarify the type or types of appeal that Paine uses and the effect he hopes to have on the audience.*

1. Tyranny, like hell, is not easily conquered; yet we have this consolation with us, that the harder the conflict, the more glorious the triumph. What we obtain too cheap, we esteem too lightly; 'tis dearness only that gives everything its value.

   _____
   _____
   _____

2. I turn with the warm ardor of a friend to those who have nobly stood, and are yet determined to stand the matter out: I call not upon a few, but upon all; not on *this* state or *that* state, but on *every* state.

   _____
   _____
   _____

3. Not all the treasurers of the world, so far as I believe, could have induced me to support an offensive war, for I think it murder; but if a thief breaks into my house, burns and destroys my property, and kills or threatens to kill me, or those that are in it, and to "*bind me in all cases whatsoever,*" to his absolute will, am I to suffer it? . . . If we reason to the root of things we shall find no difference; neither can any just cause be assigned why we should punish in the one case and pardon in the other.

   _____
   _____
   _____

Name _____ Date _____

The Declaration of Independence by Thomas Jefferson
from The Crisis, Number 1 by Thomas Paine
Reading Strategy: Recognizing Charged Words

Charged words evoke an emotional response that can make writing more memorable. Charged words are especially useful in making persuasive writing more forceful. In *The Crisis*, for example, Thomas Paine uses many negatively charged words to attack the British monarchy:

> I cannot see on what grounds the king of Britain can look up to heaven for help against us: a *common murderer*, a *highwayman*, or a *housebreaker*, has as good a pretense as he.

A. DIRECTIONS: *Underline the charged words in these sentences. Then, on the lines provided, briefly explain the emotional response each word evokes.*

1. "But when a long train of abuses and usurpations, pursuing invariably the same object, evinces a design to reduce them under absolute despotism. . . ."
   _____
   _____
   _____

2. "He has refused his assent to laws the most wholesome and necessary for the public good."
   _____
   _____
   _____

3. "In every stage of these oppressions we have petitioned for redress in the most humble terms."
   _____
   _____
   _____

4. "Tyranny, like hell, is not easily conquered."
   _____
   _____
   _____

5. "I turn with the warm ardor of a friend to those who had nobly stood, and are yet determined to stand the matter out."
   _____
   _____
   _____

Name _____ Date _____

The Declaration of Independence by Thomas Jefferson
from **The Crisis, Number 1** by Thomas Paine
Vocabulary Builder

Using the Root -fid-

A. DIRECTIONS: *The Latin root -fid- means "faith" or "trust." For each sentence that follows, use the context plus your understanding of the root -fid- to determine the meaning of the word in italics. Write the meaning on the lines after the sentence.*

1. Tamara raised her hand because she was *confident* she knew the answer.

2. In the wedding ceremony, the bride and groom vow *fidelity* to one another.

3. The information you give your doctor is *confidential* and will not be revealed to others.

4. The guardian kept his ward's bank savings in a *fiduciary* fund.

Using the Word List

unalienable	perfidy	magnanimity	acquiesce	infidel
usurpations	redress	consanguinity	impious	

B. DIRECTIONS: *Circle the letter of the pair of words that expresses a relationship most similar to the relationship of the pair in CAPITAL LETTERS.*

1. BULLY : MAGNANIMITY ::
   A. hero : courage
   B. soldier : march
   C. relative : consanguinity
   D. miser : generosity

2. LOYALTY : PERFIDY ::
   A. anger : fury
   B. kindness : cruelty
   C. soldier : march
   D. courtesy : manners

3. INFIDEL : RELIGION ::
   A. orphan : parents
   B. librarian : data
   C. priest : prayers
   D. tyrant : usurpations

4. ACQUIESCE : NOD ::
   A. delight : frown
   B. shiver : freeze
   C. approve : applaud
   D. refuse : gesture

Name _____ Date _____

The Declaration of Independence by Thomas Jefferson
from The Crisis, Number 1 by Thomas Paine
Grammar and Style: Parallelism

Parallelism is the repetition of words, phrases, or clauses with similar grammatical structures or meanings. Like all forms of repetition, it helps emphasize ideas and make them more memorable. In each example, notice how the parallel use of words, phrases, or clauses sets up a balance and rhythm that makes the sentence more emphatic and memorable.

Parallel words (adjectives):	He has called together legislative bodies at places *unusual, uncomfortable,* and *distant* from the depository of their public records.
Parallel phrases:	He has constrained our fellow citizens taken captive on the high seas *to bear arms against their country, to become the executioners of their friends and brethren,* or *to fall themselves by their hands.*
Parallel clauses:	*The harder the conflict* [is], *the more glorious the triumph* [is]. [In both clauses, the verb *is* is understood.]

A. PRACTICE: *Each of the following sentences contains at least one example of parallelism. Use a single underscore to identify the first example in a sentence, double underscores to identify a second example in the same sentence, and triple underscores to identify a third example, if any.*

1. We hold these truths to be self-evident: that all men are created equal; that they are endowed by their creator with certain inalienable rights; that among these are life, liberty and the pursuit of happiness.

2. It is the right of the people to alter or to abolish it, and to institute new government, laying its foundation on such principles and organizing its power in such form, as to them shall seem most likely to affect their safety and happiness.

3. As free and independent states, they have full power to levy war, conclude peace, contract alliances, establish commerce, and to do all other acts and things which independent states may of right do.

B. Writing Application: *Rewrite the following sentences so that all elements are parallel.*

1. The delegates pledge their lives, the fortunes they have made, and their honor, a sacred thing.
   _____
   _____

2. Jefferson criticizes the king for taking away colonial charters, the abolishment of colonial laws, and altering the colonial government.
   _____
   _____

Name _____ Date _____

The Declaration of Independence by Thomas Jefferson
from **The Crisis, Number 1** by Thomas Paine

Support for Writing

Jefferson and Paine wrote to persuade their listeners. Think of a situation in your school that you believe should be changed. To prepare for writing a **persuasive proposal** to your principal that will identify the problem and present a solution, collect your ideas in the graphic organizer below.

Proposal to Change _____

Problem: Main Statement

Problem: Details (use negative language)

Solution: Main Statement

Solution: Details (use positive language)

On a separate page, draft a persuasive proposal to your principal, defining the problem and outlining your solution. When you revise your draft, be sure to use language with negative and positive connotations, just as Jefferson and Paine did.

Name _____ Date _____

The Declaration of Independence by Thomas Jefferson
from The Crisis, Number 1 by Thomas Paine
Support for Extend Your Learning

Listening and Speaking

As you prepare two **news reports** to describe the signing of the Declaration of Independence—one to be published in the colonies and one to be published in London—follow these tips: Include the facts of the events, and consider what the news means to each audience.

   Present both news reports to students. Ask students acting as "colony" listeners to respond to the London report, and ask students acting as "London" listeners to respond to the report printed in the colonies.

Research and Technology

To prepare a **précis,** or a concise summary, of Thomas Paine's contributions to the Revolutionary cause, do research on the Internet and in the library. Enter your findings in the chart below.

Thomas Paine's Contributions to the American Revolution	
Paine's Ideas	
Paine's Actions	
Paine's Contributions to the Revolution	

   On a separate page, write your summary, or précis, of Thomas Paine's contributions to, and his effect on, the American Revolution.

Unit 2 Resources: A Nation Is Born

Name _____ Date _____

The Declaration of Independence by Thomas Jefferson
from The Crisis, Number 1 by Thomas Paine
Enrichment: Local Newspaper Editorial

Both of these selections are examples of persuasive documents that rallied people in the authors' communities to a cause. *The Crisis, Number 1,* is the more direct, personal, and emotional of the documents. The Declaration of Independence is more sober and reasonable. Yet both, in their own way, seek to persuade their audience to support the same cause—the struggle for American independence.

DIRECTIONS: *Think about your own community. Is there something you feel calls for community action or needs community support to be changed? Perhaps an old building needs restoration, or a vacant lot could be cleaned up and turned into an in-line skating area. Maybe your neighborhood needs a low-cost health clinic. Choose a cause that you would like to support. Then consider the two persuasive documents you have read and decide which approach (emotional, or calm and logical) you think will be more effective in rallying people to your cause. Keeping your approach in mind, write an editorial for the local newspaper to persuade readers to join in the action you recommend. Your editorial should be short and to the point, but you will need to write it on another sheet of paper. Plan your editorial on the following lines.*

Subject of Editorial _____

_____

Suggested Action to Take _____

_____

_____

Events or Conditions That Support the Action _____

_____

_____

_____

_____

_____

_____

_____

_____

_____

_____

_____

_____

The Declaration of Independence by Thomas Jefferson
from **The Crisis, Number 1** by Thomas Paine
Selection Test A

Critical Reading *Identify the letter of the choice that best answers the question.*

___ 1. What is Jefferson's main form of persuasion in The Declaration of Independence?
   A. He has an unusual view of how government should work.
   B. He understands that the colonists should explain their actions.
   C. He offers a list of colonists' complaints against the British king.
   D. He asks colonists to contribute their fortunes to the cause.

___ 2. Which phrase from The Declaration of Independence is charged, or filled with emotion?
   A. "for the public good"
   B. "without consent"
   C. "death, desolation, and tyranny"
   D. "in the most humble terms"

___ 3. Why is Jefferson's list of self-evident truths effective in The Declaration of Independence?
   A. It helps his audience understand him.
   B. It restates beliefs people already have.
   C. It tells people about Jefferson's beliefs.
   D. It outlines a new vision of freedom.

___ 4. What overall announcement does The Declaration of Independence make?
   A. The colonists share news of the war with Great Britain.
   B. The colonists refuse to pay unfair taxes to Great Britain.
   C. The colonists declare a separation from Great Britain.
   D. The colonists sign new agreements with Great Britain.

___ 5. In *The Crisis, Number 1*, what concern does Paine express about "the sunshine patriot" who might "shrink from the service of his country"?
   A. He wants people to live in the colonies during the summer months.
   B. He wants people to leave the colonies and go to Britain.
   C. He wants people to be willing to fight, even at great risk.
   D. He wants people to be training to be soldiers all year.

Name _____ Date _____

___ 6. In *The Crisis, Number 1*, what does Paine try to convince his listeners to fight for?
   A. property
   B. lower taxes
   C. trade items
   D. freedom

___ 7. Where does Paine use charged words in these examples from *The Crisis, Number 1*?
   A. He says he has "little superstition."
   B. He says it does not matter "what rank of life you hold."
   C. He says "Tyranny" is like "Hell."
   D. He says men know the difference between "temper" and "principle."

___ 8. In *The Crisis, Number 1*, when Paine compares the colonies' relationship with Britain to the chains of slavery, what emotion does he hope to persuade his readers to feel?
   A. anger
   B. hope
   C. confusion
   D. relief

___ 9. Why does Paine write in *The Crisis, Number 1*, that a generous parent would say: "If there must be trouble let it be in my day, that my child may have peace"?
   A. to fight now so that their descendants will not have to
   B. to put off the fight until their descendants are grown
   C. to avoid having to fight, to protect their descendants
   D. to ignore the problem altogether and hope for the best

___ 10. Which phrase from *The Crisis, Number 1* includes charged words?
   A. The heart that feels
   B. will curse his cowardice
   C. shrinks back at a time
   D. and made *them* happy

___ 11. What is the main idea of Paine's essay *The Crisis, Number 1*?
   A. The King of England is a criminal.
   B. British people must return to England.
   C. The colonists must pay taxes.
   D. The colonists must fight tyranny.

Unit 2 Resources: A Nation Is Born
© Pearson Education, Inc., publishing as Pearson Prentice Hall. All rights reserved.

Vocabulary and Grammar

___ 12. In which of the following sentences is the meaning of the word *perfidy* suggested?
   A. The Declaration lists the colonists' complaints.
   B. The Declaration suggests that the king has betrayed the colonists' trust.
   C. The Declaration sets out a vision of what makes a good government.
   D. The Declaration explains why the colonists seek independence.

___ 13. Which of the following phrases uses parallel construction?
   A. "He has forbidden his governors to pass laws of immediate and pressing importance . . ."
   B. "it becomes necessary for one people to dissolve the political bands which have connected them with another, . . ."
   C. "that all men are created equal; that they are endowed by their Creator with certain unalienable rights; that among these rights . . ."
   D. "He has erected a multitude of new offices, and sent higher swarms of officers to harass our people . . ."

Essay

14. Suppose you are a colonist who does not want or believe in independence from Great Britain, and you have just read The Declaration of Independence. Write a brief essay that gives your reasons for staying connected to the power of Britain.

15. In his opening lines of *The Crisis,* Paine says, "the harder the conflict, the more glorious the triumph." What do you think he means by these words? Do you agree with them? Write a brief essay giving your ideas about whether this phrase makes good sense to you as a way for Paine to get colonists to fight against England.

Name _____ Date _____

The Declaration of Independence by Thomas Jefferson
from The Crisis, Number 1 by Thomas Paine
Selection Test B

Critical Reading *Identify the letter of the choice that best completes the statement or answers the question.*

____ 1. What general observation does Paine express in the statement, "What we obtain too cheap, we esteem too lightly"?
   A. When something is hard to do, the achievement will be less rewarding.
   B. If you gain something too easily, it will not seem that important to you.
   C. Those who are wealthy can afford to be choosy.
   D. When your cause is just, there is no reason not to pursue it to the end.

____ 2. When Paine compares America's relationship with England to the bondage of slavery, to what emotion is he appealing?
   A. anger
   B. joy
   C. happiness
   D. hope

____ 3. Paine's primary purpose in saying that "a common murderer, a highwayman, or a housebreaker, has as good a pretense" as the king is to
   A. show how the common criminal is persecuted by the king's representatives.
   B. emphasize the notion of democracy.
   C. stress the lawlessness of the king's actions.
   D. appeal to his audience's fear of crime.

____ 4. Identify one reason Paine gives for supporting the fight for liberty.
   A. faith that God will reward the weak and powerless
   B. responsibility to ensure that all people are treated equally
   C. shame that the colonies have been afraid to break away from Britain
   D. duty to provide a better life for one's family

____ 5. What is the main point of Paine's essay?
   A. The time for armed struggle is over.
   B. Colonists who support Britain are weak and cowardly.
   C. The king of Britain is a fool.
   D. The colonists must endure.

____ 6. With what does Paine compare America's war against the British?
   A. murder
   B. all the treasures of the world
   C. a man defending his property
   D. a thief breaking into his house

Name _____ Date _____

_____ 7. Paine uses "summer soldier" and "sunshine patriot" to refer to
   A. those who support the Revolution only when it is convenient.
   B. revolutionary soldiers who keep their spirits up.
   C. agricultural workers who have joined the revolutionary army.
   D. Tories.

_____ 8. Which of the following passages from *The Crisis, Number 1*, introduces an anecdote meant to persuade the audience?
   A. "I have as little superstition in me as any man living."
   B. "[A] noted one, who kept a tavern at Amboy, was standing at his door, with as pretty a child in his hand."
   C. "The far and the near, the home counties and the back, the rich and the poor, will suffer or rejoice alike."
   D. "'Tis the business of little minds to shrink."

_____ 9. From Jefferson's statement that governments are instituted to secure basic human rights, the argument logically follows that
   A. Any form of government that suppresses people's freedoms should be overthrown.
   B. monarchy is a bad form of government because rulers are not elected.
   C. the rights of men should be supported over those of women.
   D. all forms of government destroy human rights and thus should be abandoned.

_____ 10. From the Declaration of Independence, what can be inferred about Jefferson's general attitude toward revolution?
   A. All cases of injustice vindicate a revolution.
   B. People often revolt as their first course of action.
   C. Revolution is a method of last resort.
   D. Revolution is a very poor way of dealing with conflict.

_____ 11. Jefferson uses the charged word *tyrant* to characterize the king of Britain. To what emotion does this word appeal?
   A. sorrow
   B. envy
   C. anger
   D. pride

_____ 12. Which of the following statements most appeals to the emotions of horror and disgust?
   A. "He is at this time transporting large armies . . . to complete the works of death, desolation, and tyranny, already begun."
   B. "He has abdicated government here, by declaring us out of his protection and waging war against us."
   C. "He has dissolved representative houses repeatedly. . . ."
   D. "He has called together legislative bodies . . . for the sole purpose of fatiguing them into compliance with his measures."

____ 13. Jefferson's list of self-evident truths is effective because it
   A. helps his audience understand the truths.
   B. creates a connection between these truths and the colonists' attempts at reconciliation with Britain.
   C. draws his readers' attention to his personal opinions about humanity.
   D. imparts a sense of reasonableness to the beginning of his argument.

Vocabulary and Grammar

____ 14. Which of these sentences contains examples of parallelism?
   A. "He has plundered our seas, ravaged our coasts, burned our towns, and destroyed the lives of our people."
   B. "In every stage of these oppressions we have petitioned for redress in the most humble terms."
   C. "He has kept among us in times of peace standing armies without the consent of our legislatures."
   D. "He has abdicated government here, by declaring us out of his protection and waging war against us."

____ 15. What does Jefferson mean when he says that the British are "deaf to the voice of . . . consanguinity"?
   A. They do not follow the teaching of religion.
   B. They take no account of their kinship with the colonists.
   C. They enjoy being tyrannical.
   D. They are too busy to listen to the colonists.

Essay

16. On July 8, 1776, the Declaration of Independence was read to a crowd of people standing outside the Pennsylvania State House in Philadelphia. Imagine that you are an ordinary American man or woman in the crowd. What would your reaction be? Write an essay describing your feelings about the Declaration. Give reasons for those feelings.

17. Although *The Crisis, Number 1,* was written in response to a specific situation, Paine's argument has more general applications. Write an essay in which you explore the general applications of Paine's message and discuss how the existence of more universal applications contribute to the value of Paine's essay as a work of literature.

18. When writing a persuasive essay or speech, writers often use parallelism to emphasize important ideas, create rhythm, and make their writing more forceful and direct. Write an essay in which you examine Jefferson's use of parallelism in the Declaration of Independence and analyze how it contributes to the document's effectiveness.

"An Hymn to the Evening" and "To His Excellency, General Washington"
by Phyllis Wheatley
Vocabulary Warm-up Word Lists

Study these words from the selections. Then, complete the activities.

Word List A

soothe [SOOTH] *v.* to bring comfort, composure, or relief
　The medicine helped soothe the pain in her tooth.

deforms [di FAWRMZ] *v.* spoils the appearance or function of something; disfigures
　Heat from the spotlights deforms chocolate sculptures in the candy competition.

refined [ree FYND] *adj.* Free from coarseness or vulgarity; polite
　The girl had a refined way of speaking and never used vulgar language.

majestic [mah JES tik] *adj.* possessing stateliness or grandeur
　The estate had majestic gardens that were often featured in magazines.

implore [im PLAWR] *v.* to beg for; to entreat
　After losing his sister's CD, the boy had to implore her forgiveness.

realms [RELMZ] *n.* fields or spheres; domains
　The art professor was an expert in two realms: modern painting and modern sculpture.

proceed [proh SEED] *v.* to continue, especially after an interruption
　After a lunch break, the students will proceed with the essay portion of the exam.

destined [des TIND] *v.* assigned for a specific end, use, or purpose
　The money they saved was destined for their trip to Europe.

Word List B

pealing [PEEL ing] *v.* sounding loudly and deeply
　The pealing bells summoned the entire campus to the university chapel.

exhales [eks HAYL] *v.* emits; to breathe out
　The old furnace exhales a lot of messy soot along with the hot air.

surges [SURJZ] *n.* swells or sudden increases
　Electrical surges can cause problems for computers, even though the bursts of power are short.

array [uh RAY] *n.* splendid attire; finery
　The bright array of costumes in the parade drew applause from the crowd.

martial [MAHR shel] *adj.* relating to war or the armed services
　The military school's band specializes in martial music.

drowsy [DROW zee] *adj.* sleepy; sluggish
　The toddler was drowsy after her bath, and went right to sleep.

prevail [pri VAYL] *v.* to win control; to succeed or persist
　Everyone likes to believe that justice will prevail and the innocent will be freed.

boundless [BOWND lis] *adj.* being without limits; infinite
　Cheerleaders need boundless enthusiasm and stamina to last an entire game.

Name _____ Date _____

"An Hymn to the Evening" and "To His Excellency, General Washington"
by Phyllis Wheatley
Vocabulary Warm-up Exercises

Exercise A *Fill in the blanks, using each word from Word List A only once.*

In the early 1800s, American sailors began creating scrimshaw by carving designs on the surface of the teeth and bones of whales. This was a leisure activity used to [1] _____ the nerves of the whalers confined to ships on long voyages into unknown [2] _____. Since the blubber harvested from the [3] _____ sperm whale was boiled to make lamp oil, using the ivory was a logical next step. Learning as they carved, the whalers would etch pictures of their ship, or [4] _____ with crude portraits of themselves or their sweethearts. They'd also write prayers to [5] _____ their families not to forget them. Although lack of skill clearly distorts or [6] _____ some images, others are quite accurate. Whether primitive or [7] _____, scrimshaw was [8] _____ to be prized by collectors for many years to come.

Exercise B *Answer each question in a complete sentence. Use a word from Word List B to replace each underlined word or group of words without changing its meaning.*

Example: The church had <u>loud and deep sounding</u> bells that rang every Sunday morning.
The church had <u>pealing</u> bells that rang every Sunday morning.

1. The yoga teacher <u>breathes out</u> slowly while she stretches.
_____

2. The customers came to the refreshment stands in <u>waves</u> before each movie.
_____

3. Looking down from the window of the jet, the ocean appeared <u>limitless</u>.
_____

4. The museum had an entire section devoted to books on subjects <u>about warfare</u>.
_____

5. She drove for three hours to get to the concert and was so <u>sleepy</u> when it began, she had to struggle to stay awake.
_____

6. In order to <u>triumph</u> over his opponent, the congressman campaigned heavily.
_____

7. Jockeys wear colorful silk <u>finery</u> to make their horses stand out during a race.
_____

"An Hymn to the Evening" and "To His Excellency, General Washington"
by Phyllis Wheatley
Reading Warm-up A

Read the following passage. Pay special attention to the underlined words. Then, read it again, and complete the activities. Use a separate sheet of paper for your written answers.

The American Bald Eagle, the Liberty Bell, and the Stars and Stripes are popular symbols of the United States. Each symbol reflects unique beliefs and values that the United States presents to the rest of the world.

The majestic American Bald Eagle, with its massive wingspan and ability to soar to great heights, is often depicted with arrows in one claw and an olive branch in the other. This is meant to represent the power and independence of the country in war and peace. In 1789, the American Bald Eagle was declared the U.S. national bird, giving it special protection in the wild and in captivity. In spite of that, its population did proceed to dwindle in both realms. This happened because pollution thins and deforms the shell of the eagle's egg. Fortunately, environmentalists joined together to implore the government to pass regulations eliminating the pesticides that caused the damage. As a result of their action, the eagle is no longer on the endangered species list.

Another recognizable sign of the United States is the Liberty Bell. Even though the bell cracked after it arrived, it was repaired twice and rung when the Continental Congress signed the Declaration of Independence in 1776. Because the bell was linked to that moment in history, it was destined to symbolize freedom's triumph in spite of hardships.

The Stars and Stripes are the most recognizable symbol of the United States. Because of the many people who died defending it, reverence is expected when handling the flag. There is a refined code of conduct that applies to all flag ceremonies. When a member of the armed forces dies, a flag is presented to the next of kin. The gesture is meant to show gratitude for their military service, and to soothe the family's grief.

1. Circle the words that describe the American eagle as majestic. Give an example of something you think is *majestic*.

2. Explain what *proceed* means.

3. Circle the words in the paragraph that tell in what realms the eagle population dwindled. Then, explain what *realms* means.

4. Circle the words that explain what deforms the eagle's egg. Then, tell what *deforms* means.

5. Who did the environmentalists implore? Explain what *implore* means.

6. Circle the words that explain why the Liberty Bell was destined to symbolize freedom's triumph. Then, tell what *destined* means.

7. Circle the words that tell why a refined code of conduct is expected when handling the American flag. Then, explain what *refined* means.

8. Circle the words that tell what might soothe a family's grief. Then, tell what *soothe* means.

"An Hymn to the Evening" and "To His Excellency, General Washington"
by Phyllis Wheatley

Reading Warm-up B

Read the following passage. Pay special attention to the underlined words. Then, read it again, and complete the activities. Use a separate sheet of paper for your written answers.

Besides being a founding father of the United States, Benjamin Franklin was an inventor, a scientist, a writer, and a diplomat. Although he lived before, during, and after the revolution, rather than concerning himself with martial matters, he concentrated on systems such as the post office, libraries, and fire rescue squads.

Despite his travels abroad, Franklin dressed liked a rustic, avoiding the powdered wigs and fine array that other prominent men of the time wore. His boundless imagination led to inventions and concepts that still prevail today. For example, bifocal glasses, daylight savings time, the odometer, lightning rods, the Franklin stove, and printing press were all his ideas.

In the 1700s, when Franklin lived, most American houses were made of wood and heated by fireplaces. Because the chimney exhales so much heat, Franklin devised an iron stove with a flu to keep more warmth inside the home. It was also safer. Often people tending open flames became drowsy and failed to notice sparks that could set their homes ablaze.

Franklin also found of way to protect buildings from the fires started by lightning. He attached an iron rod onto the roof of the building. Then, he attached a metal cable to the rod, and buried the cable in the ground. The rod would attract and channel the surges of electricity that formed lightning, and render them harmless.

While he was postmaster, Franklin wanted to determine the length of certain delivery routes. To do that, he created an odometer, a device that would measure and record distance by counting the rotations of a wheel's axle. After a certain number of rotations, the odometer triggered bells that could be heard pealing in the postal wagon. This sound kept the driver aware of how far he had traveled.

By his own example, Franklin demonstrated that a poor American could educate himself and become a famous citizen of the world.

1. Circle the words that tell what Franklin concentrated on instead of martial matters. Then, explain what *martial* means.

2. Tell what fine array might look like in the colonial times.

3. Why was Franklin's imagination considered boundless? Tell what *boundless* means.

4. Circle Franklin's inventions that prevail today. Then, tell what *prevail* means.

5. Circle the words that tell what the chimney exhales. Then, tell what *exhales* means.

6. Rewrite the sentence using a synonym for drowsy.

7. Tell what kind of surges are attracted to a lightning rod. Then, explain what *surges* are.

8. Rewrite the sentence using a synonym for pealing.

Name _____ Date _____

"An Hymn to the Evening" and "To His Excellency, General Washington"
by Phillis Wheatley

Literary Analysis: Personification

Personification is a figure of speech that attributes human powers and characteristics to something that is not human, such as an object, an aspect of nature, or an abstract idea. For example, in the sentence "The room waited patiently for laughter to return," the human characteristic of patience is attributed to the room.

DIRECTIONS: *On the lines after each quotation from "To His Excellency, General Washington," explain what is being personified and what human characteristic or characteristics it is being given.*

1. "See mother earth her offspring's fate bemoan."
   _____
   _____
   _____
   _____

2. "And nations gaze at scenes before unknown."
   _____
   _____
   _____
   _____

3. "Muse! bow propitious while my pen relates. . . ."
   _____
   _____
   _____
   _____

4. "Or thick as leaves in Autumn's golden reign."
   _____
   _____
   _____
   _____

5. "One century scarce perform'd its destined round."
   _____
   _____
   _____
   _____

Name _____ Date _____

"An Hymn to the Evening" and "To His Excellency, General Washington"
by Phillis Wheatley
Reading Strategy: Clarify Meaning

All writing is easier to understand if you check the definitions of unfamiliar words. In addition, poetry is often clearer if you rearrange the words into more normal grammatical structures. For example, instead of using regular subject-verb order, poetry sometimes inverts the order, placing the subject after the verb: *Wherever shines this native of the skies*. Rearranging the words into a more usual order can help you understand the poem's meaning: *Wherever this native of the skies shines*.

A. DIRECTIONS: *Clarify the meaning of these lines from the poems by rewriting them in more normal word order. Also substitute a simpler or more modern word or phrase for each word in italics. Use the context or a dictionary to help you define the italicized words.*

1. Columbia's scenes of glorious *toils* I write.

2. While freedom's cause her anxious breast *alarms*

3. As when *Eolus* heaven's fair face *deforms*

4. Where high *unfurl'd* the *ensign* waves in air

5. Shall I to Washington their praise *recite*?

6. Hear every tongue *thy guardian* aid *implore*!

7. From the *zephyr's* wing *exhales* the *incense* of the blooming spring.

8. Soft *purl* the streams

9. And through the air their *mingled* music floats.

10. So may our breasts with *ev'ry* virtue glow.

Name _____ Date _____

"An Hymn to the Evening" and "To His Excellency, General Washington"
by Phillis Wheatley
Vocabulary Builder

Using the Prefix re-

A. Directions: *The prefix* re- *can mean "again" or "back." For each sentence that follows, use the context plus your understanding of the prefix* re- *to determine the meaning of the word in italics. Write the meaning on the lines after the sentence.*

1. The government began an environmental cleanup to *reclaim* the land.
   _____
   _____

2. She quickly *rebounded* from the illness and came back to work.
   _____
   _____

Using the Word List

| celestial | propitious | pensive | scepter |
| refulgent | refluent | placid | |

B. Directions: *After each line from the poem, two possible definitions are given in parentheses for the word in italics. Underline the correct definition.*

1. *Celestial* choir! enthroned in realms of light. (heavenly, off-key)
2. She flashes dreadful in *refulgent* arms. (bad smelling, shining)
3. Muse! bow *propitious* while my pen relates. (rude, favorable)
4. The *refluent* surges beat the pounding shore. (flowing back, stagnant)
5. Anon Britannia droops the *pensive* head. (lighthearted, thoughtful)
6. Let *placid* slumbers soothe each weary mind. (mysterious, calm)
7. Night's leaden *scepter* seals my drowsy eyes. (rod or staff, cynic)

C. Directions: *Circle the letter of the word that best completes each sentence.*

1. She studied the sky at night to observe _____ bodies.
   A. celestial   C. refluent
   B. propitious   D. pensive

2. A scepter would most likely be seen in a king's or queen's _____.
   A. boot   C. last will and testament
   B. fur-lined cape   D. hand

Name _____   Date _____

"An Hymn to the Evening" and "To His Excellency, General Washington"
by Phillis Wheatley

Grammar and Style: Subject and Verb Agreement

Verb forms should agree with their subjects in number. Singular subjects take singular verb forms: *She runs.* Plural subjects take plural verb forms: *They run.*

A. Practice: *In each sentence from Wheatley's poems, underline the subject once and the verb twice. Then circle* singular *or* plural *to indicate the number of the subject and verb.*

1. She flashes dreadful in refulgent arms.   SINGULAR   PLURAL
2. And nations gaze at scenes before unknown.   SINGULAR   PLURAL
3. Unnumbered charms and recent graces rise.   SINGULAR   PLURAL
4. The refluent surges beat the sounding shore.   SINGULAR   PLURAL
5. In bright array they seek the work of war.   SINGULAR   PLURAL
6. Anon Britannia droops the pensive head.   SINGULAR   PLURAL
7. From the zephyr's wing exhales the incense of the blooming spring.   SINGULAR   PLURAL
8. Beauteous dyes are spread.   SINGULAR   PLURAL
9. The west glories in the deepest red.   SINGULAR   PLURAL
10. Night's leaden scepter seals my drowsy eyes.   SINGULAR   PLURAL

B. Writing Application: *Write the correct form of the verb in parentheses.*

1. From Christopher Columbus _____ names like Columbia. (come)
2. There _____ no goddesses called Columbia in Greek or Roman mythology. (be)
3. This creation of American neoclassical writers in the era of the Revolution _____ often depicted on coins and monuments. (be)
4. Like the bald eagle, she _____ America. (represent)
5. In Wheatley's poems there often _____ the goddess Columbia. (appear)
6. One of these poems vividly _____ the goddess. (describe)
7. Several lines in this poem _____ George Washington. (praise)

Unit 2 Resources: A Nation Is Born

Name _____ Date _____

"An Hymn to the Evening" and "To His Excellency, General Washington"
by Phillis Wheatley

Support for Writing

To organize your information for the monument inscription you are writing, use a chart like the one below to list the heroic qualities—personal and professional—of the historical figure you have chosen.

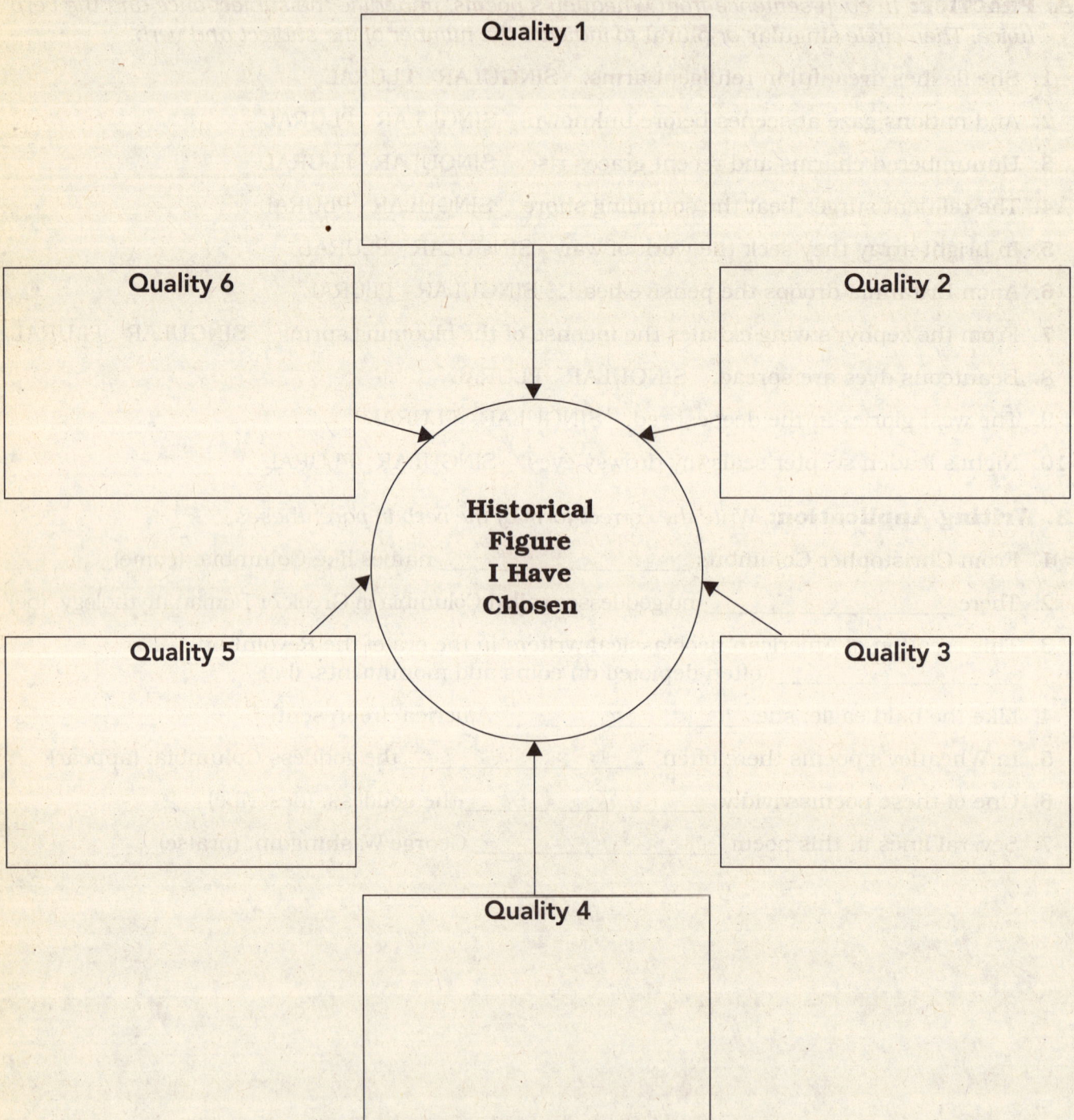

Now, use your notes to write a monument inscription honoring the person you have chosen.

Name _____ Date _____

"An Hymn to the Evening" and "To His Excellency, General Washington"
by Phillis Wheatley
Support for Extend Your Learning

Listening and Speaking

Answer these questions to organize your thoughts in preparation for a dramatic reading of one of Wheatley's poems.

1. Where are the punctuation marks, such as exclamation points, that show me where to speak louder and with more authority? _____
   _____

2. Where are the punctuation marks that tell me where to slow down or pause—dashes, commas, periods, colons, or semicolons? _____
   _____

3. Where are the elements that make the poem musical—alliteration, assonance, rhyme, and so on? _____
   _____

4. What is the meter of the poem that will guide me in reading with the proper rhythm and pace? _____
   _____

5. What parts of the poem, if any, would lend themselves to the use of body language or gestures to emphasize the drama of the passage (such as slowly lowering arm to emphasize nightfall)? _____
   _____
   _____

Research and Technology

As you gather information for your graphic display, create a graphic organizer like the one below to list the highlights of George Washington's life. Then, you can enlarge your organizer to incorporate it into your fold-out presentation poster.

Highlights of George Washington's Life

Youth	
Military Career	
Political Life	

Name _____ Date _____

"An Hymn to the Evening" and "To His Excellency, General Washington"
by Phillis Wheatley
Enrichment: Fine Art

Phillis Wheatley describes George Washington as both a military leader and a symbol of freedom. Similarly, the painting *Liberty and Washington* communicates the artists' ideas and feelings about him.

DIRECTIONS: *Reread the lines below, which express Wheatley's opinion of Washington's glory. Then compare the ways Wheatley and the artist portray Washington. Answer the questions on the lines provided.*

> Proceed, great Chief, with virtue on thy side,
> Thy ev'ry action let the goddess guide.
> A crown, a mansion, and a throne that shine,
> With gold unfading, WASHINGTON! be thine.

1. How does the painting portray Washington's military role. What is underneath Liberty's foot?
   _____

2. In your opinion, how does the painting illustrate the four lines quoted above? Why?
   _____
   _____
   _____

3. In the painting, how does color help convey the artist's attitude?
   _____
   _____
   _____

4. If you were creating a piece of visual art with George Washington as its subject, what would it be made of? What would it look like? How would it communicate your ideas and feelings about Washington? You can sketch your piece of visual art below, or you can write a description.

"An Hymn to the Evening" and **"To His Excellency, General Washington"**
by Phillis Wheatley
Selection Test A

Critical Reading *Identify the letter of the choice that best answers the question.*

___ 1. In which line does Wheatley use personification to refer to a sunset?
   A. "Soon as the sun forsook the eastern main"
   B. "Soft purl the streams, the birds renew their notes"
   C. "Let placid slumbers soothe each weary mind"
   D. "So shall the labours of the day begin"

___ 2. Which is the best clarification of the following lines?
   From the zephyr's wing, / Exhales the incense of the blooming spring.
   A. The zephyr's blooming wing exhales the incense of spring.
   B. Exhales the incense of the blooming spring from the zephyr's wing.
   C. The blooming spring exhales the incense of the zephyr's wing.
   D. The incense of the blooming spring is exhaled from the zephyr's wing.

___ 3. To whom or what does *him* refer in this lines from "An Hymn to the Evening"?
   Filled with the praise of him who gives the light;
   And draws the sable curtains of the night
   A. the west wind
   B. God
   C. George Washington
   D. placid slumbers

___ 4. Which clarification of the phrase "placid slumbers" makes the most sense?
   Let placid slumbers soothe each weary mind,
   At morn to wake more heav'nly, more refined
   A. peaceful sleep
   B. stormy passions
   C. alert wakefulness
   D. constant worries

___ 5. In "To His Excellency, General Washington," Wheatley personifies America as which goddess?
   A. Athena
   B. Britannia
   C. Columbia
   D. Eolus

___ 6. Which change would help clarify the meaning of this sentence from "An Hymn to the Evening"?

> Soft purl the streams, the birds renew their notes,
> And through the air their mingled music floats.

A. Invert the phrase "the birds renew their notes."
B. Invert the phrase "mingled music floats."
C. Invert the phrase "soft purl the streams."
D. Invert the entire sentence.

___ 7. Which statement best expresses what Wheatley means by calling America "The land of freedom's heaven-defended race"?

A. America is so weak that it needs God to defend it against its stronger enemies.
B. God watches over America because it is a free country.
C. Freedom is available only in heaven.
D. America is a heavenly country.

___ 8. Which sentence accurately clarifies the meaning of this line from "To His Excellency, General Washington"?

> Columbia's scenes of glorious toils I write.

A. Writing about Columbia is a glorious toil.
B. I write about Columbia's scenes of glorious toil.
C. I toil gloriously at writing about Columbia.
D. I write in the midst of Columbia's scenes of glorious toil.

___ 9. Who is being addressed in this sentence from "To His Excellency, General Washington"?

> Fam'd for thy valor, for thy virtues more,
> Hear every tongue thy guardian aid implore!

A. Columbia
B. Freedom
C. Eolus
D. Washington

___ 10. Which is the best way to reorder this sentence from "To His Excellency, General Washington" in order to clarify its meaning?

> Hear every tongue thy guardian aid implore!

A. Begin the sentence with *guardian*.
B. Place *implore* after *tongue*.
C. Begin the sentence with *implore*.
D. End the sentence with *guardian*.

Unit 2 Resources: A Nation Is Born

Name _____ Date _____

___ 11. Which sentence best captures the meaning of the phrase "Columbia's fury" in these lines from "To His Excellency, General Washington"?

> When Gallic powers Columbia's fury found;
> And so may you, whoever dares disgrace
> The land of freedom's heaven-defended race.

   A. Americans are quick to become angry.
   B. General Washington is like a raging storm when he charges into battle.
   C. America can be fierce in defending freedom's cause.
   D. America has gone too far in using military might against its enemies.

Vocabulary and Grammar

___ 12. Which job is concerned with *celestial* matters?
   A. gardener
   B. firefighter
   C. general
   D. astronomer

___ 13. Which word best describes a calm, still lake?
   A. refluent
   B. propitious
   C. placid
   D. refulgent

___ 14. Which sentence contains no errors in subject-verb agreement?
   A. Wheatley's poems on the subject of freedom is still very moving.
   B. Washington's comments to Wheatley shows both modesty and generosity.
   C. Many of Wheatley's poems use the literary device of personification.
   D. Wheatley's tribute to Washington and America are full of vivid images.

Essay

15. Do you think that the average American today experiences nightfall in the same way that Phillis Wheatley does in "An Hymn to the Evening"? Why or why not? Begin your essay by briefly summarizing how Wheatley portrays evening. Then, tell whether most Americans experience evening in the same way. Develop your thoughts in an essay supported by concrete examples.

16. Do you think that "To His Excellency, General Washington" and "An Hymn to the Evening" are "dated" and "out of fashion"? Or is Phillis Wheatley a poet whose works are still relevant to modern life? In an essay, state your opinion clearly. Then, support your opinion by giving details from the poems you have just read. Consider both the theme or subject matter and the style of the two poems.

Name _____ Date _____

"An Hymn to the Evening" and "To His Excellency, General Washington"
by Phillis Wheatley
Selection Test B

Critical Reading *Identify the letter of the choice that best completes the statement or answers the question.*

____ 1. At the beginning of "To His Excellency, General Washington," Wheatley portrays the United States as a goddess filled with
   A. pride.
   B. anxiety.
   C. anger.
   D. hatred.

____ 2. In "An Hymn to the Evening," the "sable curtains" refer to
   A. winter.
   B. the west wind.
   C. darkness.
   D. thunder.

____ 3. In "To His Excellency, General Washington," what human characteristics does Wheatley attribute to Great Britain?
   A. innocence and ignorance
   B. pride and vanity
   C. foolishness and greed
   D. malice and spite

____ 4. What does Wheatley imply about how others view America when she writes, "Fix'd are the eyes of nations on the scales, / For in their hopes Columbia's arm prevails"?
   A. America's fate is of little interest to the rest of the world.
   B. America has a great deal in common with the rest of the world.
   C. America's fight for freedom is a model for the rest of the world.
   D. America must win its war with Britain to justify independence.

____ 5. In "An Hymn to the Evening," Wheatley portrays night as a time of
   A. renewal.
   B. terror.
   C. virtue.
   D. death.

____ 6. In "To His Excellency, General Washington," Wheatley's use of personification is in part designed to
   A. distance the reader from the events described.
   B. make the poem more musical.
   C. help the reader recognize the beauty and strength of America.
   D. show her delight in acquiring and possessing inanimate objects.

Unit 2 Resources: A Nation Is Born
© Pearson Education, Inc., publishing as Pearson Prentice Hall. All rights reserved.

Name _____ Date _____

___ 7. In which of these instances does Wheatley use personification in "To His Excellency, General Washington"?
   A. when she says that America's armies know Washington from "fields of fight"
   B. when she compares night to a veil
   C. when she wishes that Washington could have "a crown, a mansion, and a throne that shine"
   D. when she describes England as a goddess who "droops" her "pensive head"

___ 8. Which of these quotations from "An Hymn to the Evening" illustrates personification?
   A. "But the west glories in the deepest red."
   B. "And through the air their mingled music floats."
   C. "So may our breasts with every virtue glow."
   D. "Majestic grandeur!"

___ 9. Which of the following rewritten versions clarifies this line from "To His Excellency, General Washington": "When Gallic powers Columbia's fury found"?
   A. When the French became more powerful than America's fury
   B. When the French encountered the fury of America
   C. When an angry Washington met with French government representatives
   D. When America discovered the fury and power of France

___ 10. Which of the following rewritten versions clarifies this line from "To His Excellency, General Washington": "While round increase the rising hills of dead"?
   A. While all around the number of war dead increases
   B. While the war dead killed in the hills rise and go to heaven
   C. While more vegetation on nearby hills is destroyed by warfare
   D. While the hills of dead bodies become increasingly round in shape

___ 11. Which of the following rewritten versions clarifies this line from "An Hymn to the Evening": "Soft purl the streams"?
   A. The streams ripple or murmur softly.
   B. The water softener ripples or murmurs in the streams.
   C. The water softly knits the streams together.
   D. The streams contain soft-looking water bubbles that resemble opaque white jewels.

Vocabulary and Grammar

___ 12. A *propitious* act is one that is
   A. favorable.
   B. outrageous.
   C. possessive.
   D. criminal.

___ 13. Which word could substitute for *placid* in the line "Let placid slumbers soothe each weary mind"?
   A. terrifying
   B. turbulent
   C. tranquil
   D. tired

____ 14. A *scepter* closely resembles a
   A. vase or glass.
   B. rod or staff.
   C. star or planet.
   D. god or goddess.

____ 15. In the line "Unnumber'd charms and recent graces rise," the word *rise* is a
   A. singular subject.
   B. plural subject.
   C. singular verb.
   D. plural verb.

____ 16. In the lines "The birds renew their notes, / And through the air their mingled music floats," the subject of *floats* is
   A. birds.
   B. notes.
   C. air.
   D. music.

____ 17. In the lines "From the zephyr's wing, / Exhales the incense of the blooming spring," the subject of *exhales* is
   A. wing.
   B. incense.
   C. spring.
   D. zephyr's.

Essay

18. About two-thirds of "An Hymn to the Evening" is devoted to daytime. Based on the poem, do you think Wheatley preferred the day or the night? Write an essay in which you use details from the poem to support your opinion.

19. Based on "To His Excellency, General Washington," do you think Wheatley was very patriotic? Answer this question in an essay that uses details and impressions from the poem to support your evaluation.

20. In an essay, discuss the use of General Washington as a symbol in the poem "To His Excellency, General Washington." Considering that Washington is not mentioned until line 23, is the subject of this poem something or someone other than Washington? Who or what else could be the inspiration of the poem and the subject of Wheatley's praise?

Speech in the Virginia Convention by Patrick Henry
Speech in the Convention by Benjamin Franklin

Vocabulary Warm-up Word Lists

Study these words from the selections. Then, complete the activities.

Word List A

avert [uh VERT] *v.* avoid; prevent
By following the safety rules, we will avert any disaster.

conduct [KON dukt] *n.* actions and words; behavior
The group's conduct during the field trip was excellent.

cope [KOHP] *v.* deal with problems
Marcia often cannot cope with the demands of her job.

invincible [in VIN se bel] *adj.* unconquerable; incapable of being defeated
We have won every game so far, so we feel invincible.

reconciled [RE kun syld] *v.* made friendly again; brought into harmony
The neighbors had argued for years before they were reconciled.

reserve [ree ZURV] *n.* holding back; self-control
A quiet and shy man, Stuart spoke with reserve.

revere [ree VEER] *v.* honor; admire
The people of our town respect and revere the mayor.

sentiments [SEN ti ments] *n.* feelings
Joanna has strong sentiments about keeping the environment clean.

Word List B

arduous [AR jyoo us] *adj.* difficult; challenging
They faced an arduous journey over desert and mountains.

efficiency [ee FISH en see] *n.* skill in avoiding waste
Quick service shows the efficiency of our lunchroom.

implements [IM pli ments] *n.* tools for doing work
Rakes and shovels are gardening implements.

indulge [in DULJ] *v.* yield to desires and whims; enjoy to excess
Wanting to indulge himself, Jim bought the expensive tickets.

insidious [in SID ee us] *adj.* deceitful; treacherous
An insidious plan is a mean and dangerous one.

irresolution [eer rez oh LOO shun] *n.* uncertainty; hesitation
Irresolution took over, and they were unable to make a decision.

spurned [SPURND] *v.* rejected; scorned
Spurned by the judges, Maria did not get a part in the play.

vigilant [VIJ uh lent] *adj.* alert to danger
A good watchman is vigilant.

Name _____ Date _____

Speech in the Virginia Convention by Patrick Henry
Speech in the Convention by Benjamin Franklin
Vocabulary Warm-up Exercises

Exercise A *Fill in the blanks, using each word from Word List A only once.*

Have you ever noticed how Hollywood uses the same old ideas in disaster movies? There are always some likable, ordinary people to engage the [1] _____ of the audience. There are always a few wild characters whose [2] _____ is aggressive and who throw themselves into the conflict, and other characters who act with caution and [3] _____. The writers often throw in strangers who become friends and people in conflict who become [4] _____, working together to save the day. The planet or the country or the city learns to [5] _____ with catastrophes. Everyone learns humility when they realize that, faced with the greater power of nature or space aliens, they are not [6] _____. They always [7] _____ total disaster, and along the way they acquire new heroes to [8] _____. When I become a director, I'm going to find a new way to make a disaster movie!

Exercise B *Revise each sentence so that the underlined vocabulary word is used in a logical way. Be sure to keep the vocabulary word in your revision.*

1. The group spurned the newcomer and accepted him gladly.
   _____

2. The guard was vigilant and paid no attention to his job.
   _____

3. Our group performed with great efficiency, wasting a lot of time and energy.
   _____

4. Troubled with irresolution, she took firm action immediately.
   _____

5. This arduous task is so easy you can do it with your eyes closed.
   _____

6. We have plenty of implements, and we need tools to do the job.
   _____

7. He infected our computers with an insidious virus that everyone knew about.
   _____

8. This summer, I plan to indulge in some adventure novels and not read a thing.
   _____

Name _____ Date _____

Speech in the Virginia Convention by Patrick Henry
Speech in the Convention by Benjamin Franklin

Reading Warm-up A

Read the following passage. Pay special attention to the underlined words. Then, read it again, and complete the activities. Use a separate sheet of paper for your written answers.

The Constitutional Convention, sometimes called the Philadelphia Convention, met in what is now called Independence Hall from May 25 to September 17, 1787. The conduct of the fifty-five delegates—their speeches, decisions, acts, and attitudes—set an example for the creation of a new government, an example that nations around the world continue to admire and revere.

The delegates realized that the existing Articles of Confederation formed a political structure that was far from invincible. A much stronger unifying constitution was needed. The convention delegates who created that constitution were governors, justices, attorneys, and some distinguished Americans who came out of retirement, as well as soldiers and ministers, shopkeepers and farmers. One historian called them the nation's well-bred, well-fed, well-wed, and well-read. Washington and Franklin were there; so were Hamilton and Madison. The Convention elected Washington to be its president, and they agreed to keep all proceedings secret in order to respect each delegate's thoughts and feelings. Every member could express his sentiments without reserve and discussions could be full and free.

Committees prepared drafts and worked out compromises in order to avert deadlocks. On many issues, the committees proposed a range of options so that opposing points of view could be reconciled when the delegates got together in full sessions. They had to create procedures to cope with the enormously complex array of problems they faced. Often a vote on one issue undid many days of debate on another issue, and delegates had to backtrack and reconsider issues they thought they had already solved.

The delegates designed the legislative, judicial, and executive branches of a national government. They solved the thorny problem of representation. Thirty-nine delegates signed the Constitution and sent it to the states for approval.

1. Circle the words that define **conduct**. Describe **conduct** appropriate in a classroom.

2. Underline the word that means the same as **revere**. Name someone you **revere** and tell why.

3. Circle the words that help explain **invincible**. Define **invincible** in your own words.

4. Underline the words that explain **sentiments**. Describe your **sentiments** about American literature.

5. Circle the words that mean the opposite of **reserve**. Describe a situation in which you spoke with **reserve**.

6. Underline the words that tell what the delegates did to **avert** deadlocks. Why would someone want to **avert** a standstill?

7. Circle the words that tell what as **reconciled**. Use **reconciled** in a sentence of your own.

8. Underline the words that tell what the delegates did to **cope** with problems. Name something that you **cope** with every day.

Unit 2 Resources: A Nation Is Born
© Pearson Education, Inc., publishing as Pearson Prentice Hall. All rights reserved.

Speech in the Virginia Convention by Patrick Henry
Speech in the Convention by Benjamin Franklin
Reading Warm-up B

Read the following passage. Pay special attention to the underlined words. Then, read it again, and complete the activities. Use a separate sheet of paper for your written answers.

The Bill of Rights—the first ten amendments to the Constitution—derives from the British Bill of Rights of 1689 and, ultimately, from the Magna Carta of 1215. The amendments protect individual rights from governmental abuses of power, whether violent and obvious or treacherous and insidious. The ten amendments are an American citizen's most powerful implements for building,shaping, and maintaining a truly independent political life.

The Declaration of Rights of the state of Virginia, written by George Mason, also provided a model for the federal Bill of Rights. At the Constitutional Convention, Mason suggested that such a bill would make an excellent preface to the Constitution. The majority disagreed and his idea was spurned. It was not that the delegates showed irresolution by hesitating to approve the notion. They simply thought it was unnecessary, placing their faith in the separation of powers and the checks and balances laid out in the Constitution.

Some states, however, remained uncomfortable and unconvinced. Although they admired the efficiency of the Constitution—its muscular structure with no unnecessary provisions or wasted words—they still wanted individual rights spelled out. Ultimately, only by pledging to add amendments after ratification were the supporters of the Constitution, especially James Madison, able to get it approved in some of the states. Madison's task was an arduous one, but, after great struggle, ratification was finally achieved in December 1791.

The Bill of Rights places limits on any potential attempts by the federal government to indulge in abuses of power. Over the years, the Constitution has been amended, but the Bill of Rights has not been changed. It has, of course, been debated and interpreted, but it continues to stand as a vigilant guard, watching over American freedoms.

1. Underline the word that means the same as insidious. Name something you consider *insidious* in today's world.

2. Circle the words that tell what implements do. Name three writing *implements*.

3. Underline the word that helps explain spurned. Use *spurned* in a sentence.

4. Circle the word that helps explain irresolution. Describe a situation in which *irresolution* led to a misfortune.

5. Underline the words that help explain efficiency. Explain why *efficiency* is an important element in the world of business.

6. Circle the words that explain arduous. Describe an *arduous* experience that you have had.

7. Circle the words that tell how the government might indulge itself. Use *indulge* in a sentence about maturity.

8. Underline the words that help explain vigilant. Describe a situation in which you had to remain *vigilant*.

Name _____ Date _____

"Speech in the Virginia Convention" by Patrick Henry
"Speech in the Convention" by Benjamin Franklin
Literary Analysis: Speeches

Effective **speeches** often make use of these techniques to emphasize key ideas and make them more memorable: (1) **repetition** of an idea in the same words; (2) **restatement** of a key idea in different words; (3) **parallelism,** or repeated use of the same grammatical structures; and (4) **rhetorical questions,** or questions with obvious answers that are asked not because answers are expected but to involve the audience emotionally in the speech.

DIRECTIONS: *Reread Patrick Henry's speech, and look for examples of each technique. Record the examples on the chart below.*

Restatement

Repetition

Parallelism

Rhetorical Questions

Unit 2 Resources: A Nation Is Born
© Pearson Education, Inc., publishing as Pearson Prentice Hall. All rights reserved.

Name _____ Date _____

"Speech in the Virginia Convention" by Patrick Henry
"Speech in the Convention" by Benjamin Franklin

Reading Strategy: Evaluating Persuasive Appeals

Orators often rely on **persuasive appeals** to convince an audience of their ideas. An appeal to reason calls upon the audience to think logically about an issue. An emotional appeal attempts to stir listeners by tapping into their hopes, fears, likes, and dislikes. An effective persuasive speech usually blends the two types of appeals. For example, consider Patrick Henry's famous final remark:

I know not what course others may take; but as for me, give me liberty or give me death.

Though Henry's willingness to die for the liberty he cherishes clearly makes a strong emotional appeal, the statement also makes an appeal to reason with its logical either/or structure.

DIRECTIONS: *On the lines provided, indicate whether each passage appeals to reason, emotion, or both, and explain how the passage makes each appeal.*

1. "I know of no way of judging of the future but by the past."
   _____
   _____

2. "I ask gentlemen, sir, what means this martial array, if its purpose be not to force us to submission? Can gentlemen assign any other possible motive for it?"
   _____
   _____

3. "Our petitions have been slighted; our remonstrances have produced additional violence and insult; our supplications have been disregarded; and we have been spurned with contempt from the foot of the throne! In vain, after these things, may we indulge the fond hope of peace and reconciliation."
   _____
   _____

4. "There is a just God who presides over the destinies of nations and who will raise up friends to fight our battles for us."
   _____
   _____

5. "Gentlemen may cry, 'Peace, peace,'—but there is no peace. The war is actually begun! The next gale that sweeps from the north will bring to our ears the clash of resounding arms!"
   _____
   _____

Name _____ Date _____

"Speech in the Virginia Convention" by Patrick Henry
"Speech in the Convention" by Benjamin Franklin

Vocabulary Builder

Using the Suffix -ity

A. DIRECTIONS: *The suffix -ity, meaning 'the state of,' is generally used to turn adjectives into nouns. Complete each of these sentences using the -ity noun form of one of the following adjectives:*

        complex   believable   flexible   creative   infallible

1. The realistic setting gave the story an aura of _____.
2. The _____ of the puzzle made it difficult to solve.
3. You can achieve _____ by doing stretching exercises.
4. Because of Jim's mistake, we questioned his _____.
5. The game the child invented showed imagination and _____.

Using the Word List

| arduous | subjugation | infallibility | salutary | posterity |
| insidious | vigilant | despotism | unanimity | manifest |

B. DIRECTIONS: *On the line after each pair of words, indicate whether the two words are synonyms or antonyms.*

1. devious, insidious _____
2. unwholesome, salutary _____
3. obvious, manifest _____
4. oblivious, vigilant _____
5. easy, arduous _____
6. enslavement, subjugation _____
7. dictatorship, despotism _____
8. discord, unanimity _____
9. ancestry, posterity _____
10. mistakenness, infallibility _____

Name _____ Date _____

"Speech in the Virginia Convention" by Patrick Henry
"Speech in the Convention" by Benjamin Franklin

Grammar and Style: Double Negatives

It takes only one negative word or contraction to communicate a negative idea. If you use two negatives, they logically cancel each other out, resulting in a positive statement.

Double Negative: I wo**n't never** approve it.

logically means

I may at some time approve it.

If your intention is to make a *negative* statement, you should not use a double negative. Instead, use only one negative word or contraction.

Correct Negative Form: I will **never** approve it.

or

I wo**n't ever** approve it.

Most negative words start with n—*no, not* (often contracted to **n't**), *never, none, no one, nothing, nobody,* and *nowhere,* for example. A few other words, such as *hardly, barely,* and *scarcely,* are also negatives.

A. PRACTICE: *Read the following conversation. Underline any double negatives.*

1. I'll never go to no Badgers games again.
2. Why won't you go to none of those Badgers games?
3. The Badgers don't know nothing about football!
4. That star player allows hardly no one to get in his way.
5. They play as if they haven't got no sense.
6. No one even tried to block that field goal.
7. Well, maybe it just wouldn't have done no good.

B. Writing Application: *On the lines below, Rewrite the sentences in part A that contain double negatives. Correct all the double negatives to make them acceptable usage. If a sentence is correct, write correct.*

1. _____
2. _____
3. _____
4. _____
5. _____
6. _____
7. _____

Name _____ Date _____

"Speech in the Virginia Convention" by Patrick Henry
"Speech in the Convention" by Benjamin Franklin
Support for Writing

As you prepare to write a **commentary** on a modern speech, enter information into the graphic organizer below. Be sure to focus on your opinions of the main ideas and the support for those main ideas.

On a separate page, write the first draft of your commentary. When you revise your draft, clarify your critical points. Identify how the writer succeeded or failed at supporting his or her main points.

Commentary on _____	
Title of Speech and Writer Event at which Speech Given	
Writer's Key Point 1: How point is supported/ not supported	
Writer's Key Point 2: How point is supported/ not supported	
Writer's Key Point 3: How point is supported/ not supported	

Name _____ Date _____

"Speech in the Virginia Convention" by Patrick Henry
"Speech in the Convention" by Benjamin Franklin
Support for Extend Your Learning

Listening and Speaking

Work with a group to prepare a **debate** about the value of independence or the ratification of the Constitution. First, choose students to present both sides. Choose evidence that supports your persuasive purpose, either pro or con. Include logical, ethical, and emotional appeals.

Present your group's debate to the class. Ask for feedback for both sides of the debate.

Research and Technology

To create a graphic **display** of famous speeches throughout history, consult the Internet and history books. Find several speeches from different historical periods. Find photographs and audiotapes of the presentations. Use the graphic organizer below to enter information. Use more paper if you want to include additional speeches.

Display of Famous Speeches	
Speech title and writer/ Historical time period Photograph available? Audio recording: Reader of speech	
Speech title and writer/ Historical time period Photograph available? Audio recording: Reader of speech	
Speech title and writer/ Historical time period Photograph available? Audio recording: Reading of speech	

Prepare your display and present it to the class. Keep a collection of the displays in the classroom library.

Name _____ Date _____

"Speech in the Virginia Convention" by Patrick Henry
"Speech in the Convention" by Benjamin Franklin

Enrichment: Persuasion

Patrick Henry and Benjamin Franklin were both gifted public speakers who could hold the attention of an audience and persuade listeners to accept their views. Today many politicians, religious leaders, and others in the public eye have similar talents. However, the ability to present information in a persuasive manner is also vital to less public figures, such as those involved in advertising, sales, and public relations. People in those fields regularly use most of the basic techniques of public speaking, including the four listed below.

Rhetorical questions, or questions with obvious answers, are used to make the audience feel involved, often emotionally. For example, an advertiser might ask, "Are you looking for top quality at low prices?"

Repetition, or restating the same idea in the same words, can help hammer home a point. For example, an advertiser might say, "Our prices are low, low, low!"

Restatement, or expressing the same ideas in different words, clarifies and stresses key ideas. For example, an advertiser might say, "Our prices can't be beat. No one undersells us."

Parallelism, or repeating a particular grammatical structure, helps establish a steady rhythm that makes ideas more memorable. It may also encourage an audience to accept one idea simply because it is phrased like another more acceptable idea. For example, "If you seek quality—if you like savings—then you'll love KRESTAR'S."

DIRECTIONS: *On the lines below, write a persuasive radio ad for a product that you like or a cause that you want others to support. Include at least one example of each of the four persuasive techniques described above.*

_____
_____
_____
_____
_____
_____
_____
_____
_____
_____
_____
_____

Name _____ Date _____

Speech in the Virginia Convention by Patrick Henry
Speech in the Convention by Benjamin Franklin

Selection Test A

Critical Reading *Identify the letter of the choice that best answers the question.*

___ 1. In "Speech in the Virginia Convention," Patrick Henry says, surprisingly, that he must take a certain action against England in order to be a true patriot. What is this action?
   A. support England's actions
   B. speak out against England
   C. become an officer in the army
   D. agree with the other speakers

___ 2. A rhetorical question asks a question in which the answer is already known. What would be the answer to the questions Henry asks in this passage from "Speech in the Virginia Convention"?

   And what have we to oppose them [the British government]? Shall we try argument?

   A. Yes, let us fight them with arguments.
   B. No, we should not fight against them. There is no point to it.
   C. We have nothing to fight them with, because arguments don't work.
   D. Let us try to find a new way to work together with them, if we can.

___ 3. What action does Henry want his audience to take in "Speech in the Virginia Convention"?
   A. to pay unpopular taxes
   B. to join the British Army
   C. to work for peace
   D. to fight Britain

___ 4. In "Speech in the Virginia Convention," what emotion does Henry say is natural to people but should not be trusted in dealings with Britain?
   A. anger
   B. humor
   C. hope
   D. love

___ 5. In "Speech in the Virginia Convention," which passage appeals to the reader's sense of reason?
   A. His actions are guided by "the lamp of experience."
   B. He is willing to know the truth "whatever anguish of spirit it may cause."
   C. He shouts, "I repeat it sir, we must fight!!"
   D. He tells the others he wants freedom "or . . . death!"

Name _____ Date _____

___ 6. What "storm" does Henry say approaches the new nation?
   A. British troops and warships
   B. disagreements among speakers
   C. war with Great Britain
   D. an east coast hurricane

___ 7. When Patrick Henry ends his speech with ". . . give me liberty or give me death," he repeats words. What else does he repeat in this phrase?
   A. nothing else
   B. the structure of a question followed by another question
   C. the lessons he once learned as a young man
   D. the structure of a verb followed by a pronoun and a noun

___ 8. Which statement from "Speech in the Virginia Convention" appeals to the reader's emotions?
   A. "But different men often see the same subject in different lights . . ."
   B. "The war is inevitable—and let it come! I repeat it, sir, let it come!"
   C. "I know of no way of judging the future but by the past . . ."
   D. "What terms shall we find that have not already been exhausted?"

___ 9. What does Franklin say as a sort of confession in "Speech in the Convention"?
   A. He does not completely approve of the document but supports it anyway.
   B. He was impressed that the delegates wrote the Constitution on their first try.
   C. He has never met many of the delegates but likes them now.
   D. He did not realize how smart the delegates were.

___ 10. In "Speech in the Convention," Franklin mentions a woman who says, "But I meet with nobody but myself that is *always* in the right." Which sentence is a restatement of this idea?
   A. Have I met with you before?
   B. I meet with many people who think correctly.
   C. I meet with many people each day.
   D. I never find errors in my own thinking.

___ 11. In "Speech in the Convention," why does Franklin think the delegates should keep their concerns about the Constitution to themselves?
   A. He thinks their criticisms should never have been made in the first place.
   B. He wants the public to have confidence in the government.
   C. He thinks the Constitution is perfect and needs no changes.
   D. He thinks the document will lead to a perfect form of government.

Name _____ Date _____

Vocabulary and Grammar

___ 12. In which sentence is the meaning of the word *unanimity* suggested?
   A. Franklin urged every member of the Convention to sign the Constitution.
   B. Franklin praised the high quality of the new Constitution.
   C. Franklin found he doubted his judgments more as he grew older.
   D. Franklin wanted other nations to approve of the new Constitution.

___ 13. Which of the following sentences contains a double negative?
   A. The Convention didn't create no perfect Constitutional document.
   B. The delegates never did agree on all parts of the Constitution.
   C. Franklin said he did not approve of the Constitution.
   D. Franklin urged the delegates not to vote against the new document.

Essay

14. What do you think would cause Patrick Henry to say: "Give me liberty or give me death?" Do you think this was just a phrase to inspire his listeners, or do you think he meant it? Write a brief essay to give your opinion on what might have been going through Henry's mind as he made the statement.

15. Benjamin Franklin suggests in "Speech in the Convention" that he has learned after a long life to doubt his judgment of others. What does this statement mean? Write a brief essay that explains what Franklin means, and describe how people can change as they became older.

"**Speech in the Virginia Convention**" by Patrick Henry
"**Speech in the Convention**" by Benjamin Franklin
Selection Test B

Critical Reading *Identify the letter of the choice that best completes the statement or answers the question.*

____ 1. The main purpose of Henry's speech is to
   A. convince the colonists that Britain will not fight.
   B. maintain peace in America at all costs.
   C. persuade the colonists to enter into war against Britain.
   D. persuade his audience that Henry would make a good president.

____ 2. What is the "storm" that Henry predicts is approaching?
   A. an argument during the Convention
   B. a hurricane from the south
   C. the wrath of God
   D. the war with Britain

____ 3. Which of these remarks uses logical arguments to appeal to reason?
   A. "Are we disposed to be of the number of those who having eyes see not, and having ears hear not the things which so nearly concern their temporal salvation?"
   B. "There is no retreat but in submission and slavery!"
   C. "The next gale that sweeps from the north will bring to our ears the clash of resounding arms!"
   D. "I ask gentlemen, sir, what means this martial array, if its purpose be not to force us to submission?"

____ 4. Which technique of speeches does Henry use in the sentence "Is this the part of wise men, engaged in a great and arduous struggle for liberty?"
   A. repetition
   B. parallelism
   C. rhetorical question
   D. restatement

____ 5. In which of these statements does Henry use parallelism?
   A. "Mr. President, it is natural to man to indulge in the illusions of hope."
   B. "We have petitioned; we have remonstrated; we have supplicated."
   C. "Is it that insidious smile with which our petition has been lately received?"
   D. "Our brethren are already in the field! Why stand we here idle?"

____ 6. Henry uses a rational argument to convince his readers that
   A. chains and slavery will be the result of continued inaction by the colonies.
   B. the war is inevitable and the colonies must fight.
   C. the past conduct of the British government proves that England has no intention of granting the colonies' petitions.
   D. death would be better than a forced loss of colonial liberty.

Name _____ Date _____

____ 7. Why does Henry make use of a biblical quotation in his speech?
   A. to appeal to reason
   B. to prove his devotion to God
   C. to appeal to his audience's faith
   D. to show he has read the Bible

____ 8. In which of these sentences does Henry appeal to emotions in order to persuade his audience that the time for action is at hand?
   A. "But different men often see the same subject in different lights."
   B. "Is life so dear, or peace so sweet, as to be purchased at the price of chains and slavery?"
   C. "And in proportion to the magnitude of the subject ought to be the freedom of the debate."
   D. "I know of no way of judging the future but by the past."

____ 9. What is the main point of Benjamin Franklin's speech in the Convention?
   A. The Constitution is too weak to be approved by the Convention.
   B. His doubts about the Constitution are too strong to allow him to support it, but he hopes others will.
   C. The Convention should support the Constitution because they have shown infallibility in the past.
   D. The Convention should support the Constitution because it is as good as it is likely to be.

____ 10. Which technique of speeches does Franklin use in this passage?
   From such an assembly can a perfect production be expected?
   A. restatement
   B. repetition
   C. rhetorical question
   D. parallelism

____ 11. Why does Franklin want the delegates to the Convention to support the Constitution strongly despite any personal reservations about it?
   A. to inspire public confidence in their leadership
   B. because he believes it is perfect
   C. because that means it will be administered well
   D. because it is a product of their joint wisdom

Vocabulary and Grammar

____ 12. When Franklin hopes the Convention will "act heartily for the sake of our *posterity*," he means for the sake of
   A. immediate advantages.
   B. political leaders.
   C. fellow delegates.
   D. succeeding generations.

Name _____ Date _____

___ 13. Which of these statements contains a double negative?
   A. He was less well prepared than he should have been.
   B. She hadn't heard no bell ring.
   C. There is no better speaker than she.
   D. The people listening hardly understood what he implied.

___ 14. Which of these statements comes closest to Franklin's meaning when he says, "I am not sure that it is not the best"?
   A. "I am absolutely sure it is the best."
   B. "It may be the best."
   C. "I am not sure it is the best."
   D. "It may not be the best."

___ 15. When Franklin doubts his own *infallibility* regarding his opinion of the Constitution, he is saying that
   A. he could be wrong about it.
   B. he is unsure what his descendants will think about it.
   C. he cannot make up his mind about it.
   D. he feels compelled to vote against it.

Essay

16. Write an essay in which you examine the blend of emotional and logical appeals that Patrick Henry uses in his "Speech in the Virginia Convention" and discuss how his use of these persuasive techniques contributes to the effectiveness of the speech.

17. What is Benjamin Franklin's opinion of the Constitution? How does he reconcile this opinion with his call for the Convention delegates to give it their unanimous support? Answer these questions in an essay that supports general statements with quotations and other details from Franklin's speech.

18. When delivering a speech, a skilled orator will use a variety of oratorical devices to emphasize important points. Write an essay in which you discuss Patrick Henry's use of oratorical devices such as rhetorical questions, repetition, restatement, and parallelism in his "Speech in the Virginia Convention." In your essay, consider whether his use of these devices is effective.

Letters of Abigail Adams and Michel-Guillaume Jean de Crevecoeur
Vocabulary Warm-up Word Lists

Study these words from the selections. Then, complete the activities.

Word List A

ample [AM pel] *adj.* more than enough
　　We have an ample supply of medicine; it is more than enough for everyone.

compact [KOM pakt] *adj.* closely packed together
　　Be sure the boxes are compact, so that they take up a small space.

confer [ken FUR] *v.* give; grant
　　We confer this honor on you today in recognition of your bravery.

continual [kon TIN yoo el] *adj.* repeated often; not interrupted
　　Their continual appearances on television have made them famous.

establishment [ess TAB lish ment] *n.* a thing set up (house, business)
　　People have been buying tea at this establishment for a hundred years.

extensive [eks TEN siv] *adj.* covering a wide area; vast
　　The extensive landscape stretched out before her.

inconvenience [in ken VEEN yents] *n.* lack of comfort; trouble
　　The train delay was a major inconvenience for everyone.

metamorphosis [met e MOR foh sis] *n.* change of form or shape
　　Jon has undergone a metamorphosis since he began working out at a gym.

Word List B

accommodate [uh KOM eh dayt] *v.* make fit; allow for; have lodging for
　　This hotel can accommodate five hundred guests.

expended [eks PEN ded] *v.* used up
　　We expended all our energy getting to the top of the hill.

extricate [EKS tri kayt] *v.* set free; release; disentangle
　　Somehow I will have to extricate you from this trap!

indulgent [in DUL jent] *adj.* kind; lenient; easily giving in to desires
　　Her indulgent parents give her anything she wants.

interspersed [in ter SPURST] *v.* scattered here and there
　　Interspersed among the red roses were bright yellow daisies.

penury [PEN ye ree] *n.* poverty; lack of money or property
　　His low-paying job just barely kept him from penury.

subsistence [sub SIS tents] *n.* means of support (food, clothing, shelter)
　　Because of the harsh climate, their level of subsistence was very low.

voluntary [VOL en tair ee] *adj.* freely done or chosen
　　Your voluntary help during the crisis was deeply appreciated.

Name _____ Date _____

Letters of Abigail Adams and Michel-Guillaume Jean de Crevecoeur
Vocabulary Warm-up Exercises

Exercise A *Fill in the blanks, using each word from Word List A only once.*

Since a new restaurant called Marco's opened on our street, the old neighborhood has seen many positive changes. In fact, you could say it has experienced a genuine [1] _____. All the construction caused us some irritation and [2] _____ for a while, but dealing with the [3] _____ noise and increased traffic was worth it in the long run. From outside, the new restaurant appears to be a small, [4] _____ place, but inside there is [5] _____ room between the tables. The menu is large, offering an [6] _____ selection of many different kinds of foods. Marco's is quite a pleasant [7] _____, bustling but quiet and rather elegant. The owners seem to have tried to [8] _____ a classy atmosphere on the place, and they succeeded. They succeeded in reenergizing our neighborhood too.

Exercise B *Answer the questions with complete explanations.*

1. If you <u>extricate</u> yourself from trouble, are you still caught in a difficult situation?
   _____

2. If a supervisor is <u>indulgent</u>, does she enforce the rules too strictly?
   _____

3. If a family is concerned about its <u>subsistence</u>, what is it worried about?
   _____

4. If taking part in a holiday program is <u>voluntary</u>, can you choose whether or not to participate?
   _____

5. If a runner has <u>expended</u> his energy, how much has he saved for the end of the race?
   _____

6. If a theater has two hundred seats, how many people can it <u>accommodate</u>?
   _____

7. If, in a forest, the maple trees were <u>interspersed</u> among the oak trees, were the maples all bunched together?
   _____

8. If a man is suffering from <u>penury</u>, does he have enough money to solve his problem?
   _____

Name _____ Date _____

Letters of Abigail Adams and Michel-Guillaume Jean de Crevecoeur

Reading Warm-up A

Read the following passage. Pay special attention to the underlined words. Then, read it again, and complete the activities. Use a separate sheet of paper for your written answers.

The story of the planning of Washington, D.C. is a fascinating tale. President George Washington hired a French architect, Major Pierre Charles L'Enfant, to create a plan for the layout of the capital. L'Enfant realized that the capital could not be a compact little town but a city that would need to grow. It would change its form just as the nation itself would certainly experience a metamorphosis. Accordingly, L'Enfant's plans allowed for plenty of expansion.

L'Enfant imagined a complex including the Capitol building and an "executive mansion," an establishment that came to be known as the White House. He planned two series of broad and ample avenues that converged into circular intersections. This pattern of radiating avenues allowed for long and extensive vistas that created a sense of reaching out to great expanses.

L'Enfant, however, paid little attention to his budget or to the inconvenience of the fact that many people already owned the land he planned to build on. So Washington fired him, and he took all his plans with him back to France. Here is where the story becomes controversial. Some historians believe that Benjamin Banneker, the African American mathematician and astronomer who was an assistant surveyor on the project, reproduced L'Enfant's detailed plans from memory. Thus, the nation owes an enormous debt of gratitude to Banneker for making possible the magnificent creation of Washington, D.C.

Other historians, however, deny the accuracy of this story. They believe that this legend keeps cropping up around Banneker. It creates continual confusion about the historical truth of the event. Although the issue remains unresolved, we should still confer on Banneker credit as a surveyor of the site. We should still grant him honor as an African American who played a role in the birth of the nation's capital.

1. Circle the word that helps explain compact. Name three things that can be described as **compact**.

2. Underline the words that mean the same as metamorphosis. Describe a **metamorphosis** that you have seen.

3. Circle the words that suggest the meaning of establishment. Use **establishment** in a sentence of your own.

4. Underline the word that helps explain ample. Name three synonyms for **ample**.

5. Circle the words that help explain extensive. Describe something that is **extensive**.

6. Underline the words that explain the inconvenience ignored by L'Enfant. Define **inconvenience** in your own words.

7. Circle the words that explain continual. Name something that is a **continual** delight to you.

8. Underline the word that explains confer. Name an honor you would like someone to **confer** on you.

Letters of Abigail Adams and Michel-Guillaume Jean de Crevecoeur
Reading Warm-up B

Read the following passage. Pay special attention to the underlined words. Then, read it again, and complete the activities. Use a separate sheet of paper for your written answers.

From the time the first colonists emigrated to America to <u>extricate</u> themselves from the economic and religious entanglements of Europe, to almost the beginning of the twentieth century, farming was the essential economic enterprise in America. It was more important than the merchant trade, industry, and manufacturing. Farming began as a matter of life-or-death, and grew into the driving force of the new nation's economic life.

American agriculture flourished because of the vast tracts of fertile land on the continent, land nourished by a temperate climate. It flourished because American farmers usually owned their own land and <u>expended</u> every effort to grow all they could. Their lives as American farmers were <u>voluntary</u>; they had made their own choices, and they were inspired to succeed.

The earliest colonists realized that many European crops and methods would not work in America, so they had to discard them and <u>accommodate</u> Native American methods. Corn became the leading crop grown for food in all the colonies, although cornfields were <u>interspersed</u> with fields devoted to wheat, oats, and rye. In New England, farmers had small farms, but these hardy people avoided <u>penury</u> and even made small profits with hard work and sheer will power. In the South, tobacco, rice, and cotton were grown on plantations largely for commercial use. Almost all early American farmers were self-sufficient; beyond what they needed for their own <u>subsistence</u>, they usually raised some food and livestock for sale.

In colonial days, farmers used wooden tools that they often crafted themselves, and farm labor was intense, backbreaking, and never-ending. Farmers had to be efficient and devoted; they could not afford to be careless, undisciplined, or <u>indulgent</u>, since every part of the process—clearing land, plowing, planting, weeding, harvesting, storing, transporting—was done by manual labor. Some animals were used, but machines were still in the future.

1. Underline the word that helps explain *extricate*. Explain how you would *extricate* a bird caught in a wire fence.

2. Circle the words that tell what the farmers *expended*. What resources do you think should be *expended* to fight poverty?

3. Underline the words that explain *voluntary*. What noun is formed from the same root as *voluntary*?

4. Circle the words that tell what the colonists had to *accommodate*. Describe a situation in which you had to *accommodate* a friend.

5. Define *interspersed* in your own words, and use it in a sentence.

6. Circle the words that help explain *penury*. Name two antonyms for *penury*.

7. Identify what you think the farmers needed for their own *subsistence*.

8. Underline the words that help explain *indulgent*. Describe a situation in which you were able to be *indulgent*.

Name _____ Date _____

"Letter to Her Daughter from the New White House" by Abigail Adams
from Letters from an American Farmer by Michel-Guillaume Jean de Crèvecoeur
Literary Analysis: Private and Public Letters (Epistles)

While Abigail Adams penned a **private letter** that she intended only for her daughter, Crèvecoeur's letter qualifies as an **epistle,** a letter intended for public readership. Epistles are usually written in a style more formal than that of a personal letter. The letter form, however, allows the author to present personal ideas and opinions as if he or she were actually writing a private letter.

DIRECTIONS: *In each blank, write E if the sentence seems more likely to be found in an epistle. Write PL if the sentence seems more likely to be found in a private letter.*

_____ 1. Future generations who read this missive must recognize the dreams of our era.

_____ 2. You must visit us soon; we are all eager to see you again.

_____ 3. What a glorious sensation of self-worth overcomes them as they establish homes upon a land that is their *own!*

_____ 4. Please tell no one this secret I am about to confess.

_____ 5. Guess what? We met your sister while we were visiting the White House.

_____ 6. We must all recognize the sense of purposefulness that gives people the strength to persevere.

_____ 7. Perhaps the greatest question that each of us faces, now and in the future, is how to define and renew the American dream.

Name _____ Date _____

"Letter to Her Daughter from the New White House" by Abigail Adams
from Letters from an American Farmer by Michel-Guillaume Jean de Crèvecoeur
Reading Strategy: Distinguish Between Fact and Opinion

Opinions state personal beliefs or preference and cannot be proven. **Facts,** in contrast, can be proven. Here are examples from Adams's letter:

Fact: The river, which runs up to Alexandria, is in full view of my window.

Opinion: The house is upon a grand and superb scale.

Opinions can make writing lively and provocative, but good writers support their opinions with facts. Good readers distinguish facts from opinions and make sure they are not too easily influenced by unsupported opinions.

DIRECTIONS: *In the left column of the chart below, list the opinions the following paragraph contains. In the right column, list the facts used to support each opinion.*

Abigail Smith married John Adams, a young Boston lawyer, in 1764. During the ten years that began in 1774, Abigail's life was extraordinarily difficult. She spent most of those years apart from her husband, who was engaged in government matters in Philadelphia. In addition to raising four young children, she had to manage the family farm in her husband's absence. Meanwhile, John had become one of the infant American nation's most influential political figures, first as a member of the Continental Congress and later as second President of the United States. Abigail herself, though she had no formal education, had a voice of some importance in the new nation. An early American advocate of women's rights, she once admonished her husband to "Remember the ladies. Do not put unlimited power in the hands of husbands." She also said, "If particular care and attention is not paid to the ladies, we are determined to foment rebellion, and will not be bound by any laws in which we have no voice or representation."

OPINION	FACTS THAT SUPPORT IT

Unit 2 Resources: A Nation Is Born

Name _____ Date _____

"Letter to Her Daughter from the New White House" by Abigail Adams
from **Letters from an American Farmer** by Michel-Guillaume Jean de Crèvecoeur

Vocabulary Builder

Using Etymologies

A. DIRECTIONS: *A word's etymology, or history, can help you determine the meaning of the word today. Circle the letter of the correct meaning of each word below based on the etymology provided in brackets. In the etymologies, the symbol < means "derived from."*

1. **cot** [Middle English < Old English *cot*, "cottage"]
   A. hut   B. mansion   C. castle   D. monument

2. **parlor** [Middle English parlour < Old French *parleor* < *parler*, "to speak"]
   A. bedroom   B. bathroom   C. living room D. attic

3. **haunch** [Middle English *haunche* < Old French *hanche*, "hip"]
   A. ear   B. hoof   C. loin   D. wing

4. **frolicsome** [Dutch *vrolijk* < Middle Dutch *vrolijc*, "merry"]
   A. playful   B. forceful   C. beautiful   D. gloomy

Using the Word List

| extricate | asylum | despotic |
| agues | penury | subsistence |

B. DIRECTIONS: *Choose the word from the Word List that best completes the meaning of each sentence, and write the word on the line provided. Use each word only once.*

1. Many people, fleeing _____ treatment in other lands, have found a freer life in the United States.

2. Often they came to escape a life of _____ in which they often found it difficult to put food on the table.

3. Their poverty left them subject to _____ and other types of illness.

4. They sought to _____ themselves from their impoverished lives.

5. For such immigrants, America offered _____ from political oppression.

6. In America they could own and farm land or find other means of _____.

Name _____ Date _____

"Letter to Her Daughter from the New White House" by Abigail Adams
from **Letters from an American Farmer** by Michel-Guillaume Jean de Crèvecoeur

Grammar and Style: Semicolons

The semicolon is often used to join closely related independent clauses. Sometimes the second clause explains or elaborates on the first. For example:

Six chambers are made comfortable; two are occupied by the President and Mr. Shaw.

Sometimes the second clause presents a contrasting idea. For example:

Formerly they were not numbered in any civil lists of their country, except in those of the poor; here they rank as citizens.

A. Practice: *Read each sentence. If the semicolon connects contrasting independent clauses, write C on the line provided. If the semicolon connects two clauses in which the second explains or elaborates on the first, write E.*

_____ 1. Crèvecoeur saw America as a melting pot of different nationalities; one family he described had an English grandfather, a Dutch wife, and a French daughter-in-law.

_____ 2. Abigail Adams wrote her letter only to her daughter; Crèvecoeur addressed his epistle to the public at large.

_____ 3. Adams did not want others to learn of her criticisms of the new capital; she told her daughter to report only positive things.

_____ 4. In Europe, said Crèvecoeur, poor people were held down by "want, hunger, and war"; in America, they could become citizens and property owners.

B. Writing Application: *On the lines provided, rewrite each pair of sentences as a single sentence in which a semicolon joins related independent clauses.*

1. The White House seems superbly designed.
   Its excellent situation offers a fine view of the Potomac River.
   _____
   _____

2. The oval drawing room will be beautiful when it is completed.
   Even unfinished, it is handsome.
   _____
   _____

3. There are forests all around, but no one will cut wood.
   There is coal, but no grates to burn it in.
   _____
   _____

4. America offers asylum to the poor of Europe.
   Here, people can farm their own land.
   _____
   _____

Name _____ Date _____

"Letter to Her Daughter from the New White House" by Abigail Adams
from **Letters from an American Farmer** by Michel-Guillaume Jean de Crèvecoeur
Support for Writing

Prepare to write a **personal letter** to either Adams or Crèvecoeur, telling him or her how society has changed. First, fill in the graphic organizer below.

Letter to _____	
Person I'm writing to: Why I chose this person	
Comparison of landscape: Then and now	
Comparison of houses: Then and now	
Comparison of social life and ideas: Then and now	

On a separate page, write a draft of your letter. When you revise, remember that the person to whom you are writing lived over two centuries ago. Will he or she understand the things you are talking about? Insert specific descriptions and details to make your comparisons clear.

Unit 2 Resources: A Nation Is Born
© Pearson Education, Inc., publishing as Pearson Prentice Hall. All rights reserved.

Name _____ Date _____

"Letter to Her Daughter from the New White House" by Abigail Adams
from Letters from an American Farmer by Michel-Guillaume Jean de Crèvecoeur
Support for Extend Your Learning

Research and Technology

As your group prepares **advertisements** to draw immigrants to America in the late 1700s, keep these things in mind: Who would have been the target group for such ads? What message and images would have convinced these people to journey to a new land?

Use a software drawing program to create advertisements. Display your group's work in the classroom.

Listening and Speaking

To prepare your **role play** as three listeners to Crèvecoeur's letter, enter your responses into the graphic organizer below.

Recent immigrant to U.S. in late 1700s
Responses to Crèvecoeur letter
_____
_____
_____

Descendant of newly established, wealthy immigrant American
Responses to Crèvecoeur letter
_____
_____
_____

Poor European
Responses to Crèvecoeur letter
_____
_____
_____

Rehearse what each of you will say. Then, ask your teacher, or another student, to read a portion of the Crèvecoeur selection. Present the role play to the class.

Name _____ Date _____

"Letter to Her Daughter from the New White House" by Abigail Adams
from **Letters from an American Farmer** by Michel-Guillaume Jean de Crèvecoeur

Enrichment: Writing a Business Letter

Despite the technological advances of the past two centuries, communication through letters is still common and often necessary. Writing business letters—to request information, for example, or to thank someone for an interview—is an important workplace skill. Business letters follow certain rules or conventions that help the writer provide necessary information in a format that will be clear to the recipient. Here is a sample business letter from a job applicant.

8532 Ravenswood Road
Crofton, IN 46391

June 17, 1999

Director of Human Resources
BookWorm, Inc.
4900 West Arbor Street
Chicago, IL 60630

Dear Director of Human Resources:

    I would like to apply for the position of manager at your Lakeview store, as advertised in the June 16, 1999, issue of the *Chicago Clarion*.
    As the enclosed résumé shows, I have spent the past five years working at several Gigabook stores in the Mid-west, including two years as assistant manager of the Crofton, Indiana, store.
    Working as an assistant manager for a huge book retailer, I have handled everything from a flooded warehouse to larger-than-expected crowds at book signings. I know I would enjoy working in the smaller, more intimate setting your bookstores offer.
    Since Crofton is so close to Chicago, I can be available for an interview at any time convenient to you.
    I look forward to meeting with you.

Sincerely yours,

Peter J. Rossi

Peter J. Rossi

Encl.

Heading The address of the writer and the date

Inside Address The name (and/or title) and address of the recipient of the letter

Salutation The greeting, followed by a colon (not a comma); if you don't have the name of a particular person, use a title or the name of a department or business (*Dear Customer Relations Department; Dear Burrito Bill's*)

Body The letter's message—ideally presented in short paragraphs that are polite, brief, clear, and carefully proofread

Closing A conventional ending; other possibilities include *Respectfully* yours and *Yours truly*

Signature The signature in ink of the writer, followed by his or her typed name

Notation An indication, when appropriate, of copies sent or other materials enclosed

DIRECTIONS: *Imagine that you are reading the Sunday newspaper and come across an advertisement for your dream summer job. On a separate sheet of paper, write a letter applying for that job. Use the format shown in the sample, and be sure to proofread carefully so that your final version is free of errors. Use the space below to jot down ideas about your letter's contents.*

Name _____ Date _____

"Letter to Her Daughter from the New White House" by Abigail Adams
from **Letters from an American Farmer** by Michel-Guillaume Jean de Crèvecoeur

Selection Test A

Critical Reading *Identify the letter of the choice that best answers the question.*

___ 1. Which passage from "Letter to Her Daughter from the New White House" is an opinion?
   A. "I arrived here on Sunday last."
   B. "The river is in full view of my window."
   C. "It is a very handsome room now."
   D. "Upstairs there is the oval room."

___ 2. In "Letter to Her Daughter from the New White House," what fact does Abigail Adams offer to support her opinion that members of Congress will not find much comfort in Washington?
   A. The forests are too close to the homes.
   B. The buildings are unfinished.
   C. The roads are poorly marked.
   D. The river is in full view of her window.

___ 3. Why does Adams want bells, based on "Letter to Her Daughter from the New White House"?
   A. to heat the White House
   B. to signal for help in the White House
   C. to sing songs in the White House
   D. to amuse herself in the White House

___ 4. What does Adams ask her daughter to keep secret in "Letter to Her Daughter from the New White House"?
   A. her opinions on the city of Washington
   B. her opinions on the roads on the route
   C. her opinions on the state of the house
   D. her opinions on the people she has met

___ 5. Based on "Letter to Her Daughter from the New White House," what does Adams think of Washington so far?
   A. She thinks it needs work as a city.
   B. She thinks it is a wonderful capital.
   C. She thinks it is too close to the woods.
   D. She thinks it is too far from Baltimore.

_____ 6. Based on "Letter to Her Daughter from the New White House," which of these best describes the character of Abigail Adams?
   A. She is impressed by wealth and power.
   B. She does not trust anyone.
   C. She makes the best of any situation.
   D. She complains about everything.

_____ 7. In *Letters from an American Farmer*, which opinion does Crèvecoeur support?
   A. People can have no loyalty to a nation that cannot feed them.
   B. People can have no loyalty to a nation that does not have many kinds of people.
   C. People can have no loyalty to a nation that has no laws.
   D. People can have no loyalty to a nation that has no art.

_____ 8. Why is *Letters from an American Farmer* considered a public letter?
   A. It should be read only as a speech.
   B. It should be read by a wide audience.
   C. It should be read only by Europeans.
   D. It should be read only by Americans.

_____ 9. How does Crèvecoeur compare people to plants in *Letters from an American Farmer*?
   A. Plants' roots grow on people's farms.
   B. Both need regular food and water.
   C. Plants are food for people.
   D. Both can grow only in Europe.

_____ 10. In what way is *Letters from an American Farmer* both personal and public writing?
   A. The author's ideas are known to a large part of the reading public.
   B. The author's public ideas grow out of his own personal experience.
   C. The author's personal life has been lived mostly in the public eye.
   D. The author's ideas are meant to be read everywhere.

_____ 11. Based on *Letters from an American Farmer*, what helped Europeans become American citizens?
   A. hunger
   B. war
   C. jails
   D. hard work

Vocabulary and Grammar

____ 12. In which sentence is the meaning of the word *agues* suggested?
   A. When I had the flu, I shivered.
   B. People came to visit me.
   C. They brought me soup.
   D. I woke up feeling better.

____ 13. Which of the following sentences **correctly** uses the semicolon?
   A. I arrived here on Sunday; and without meeting with any accident.
   B. The river, which runs up to Alexandria; is in full view of my window.
   C. It is a very handsome room now; when completed, it will be beautiful.
   D. The more I view it; the more I am delighted with it.

Essay

14. Based on "Letter to Her Daughter from the New White House," what kind of person do you think Abigail Adams was? Write a brief essay giving your opinion. Use one example from the letter to support your opinion.

15. Michel-Guillaume Jean de Crèvecoeur was the first writer to compare American society with the "melting pot." What do you think this phrase means? Write a brief essay to tell what you think the "melting pot" means. Give one example from the selection to support your opinion.

Name _____ Date _____

"Letter to Her Daughter from the New White House" by Abigail Adams
from **Letters from an American Farmer** by Michel-Guillaume Jean de Crèvecoeur

Selection Test B

Critical Reading *Identify the letter of the choice that best completes the statement or answers the question.*

____ 1. What main point does Abigail Adams's description of Washington stress?
   A. her reluctance to move there
   B. the city's isolation and unfinished state
   C. the romance of her primitive surroundings
   D. the city's beauty and impressive design

____ 2. Why do you think Adams asks her daughter not to tell others the letter's revelations about the new capital?
   A. She believes only family members should have to listen to her complaints.
   B. She fears people would be appalled if they knew the true state of the capital.
   C. She realizes that her complaints stem solely from her own personal unhappiness.
   D. She recognizes that the President's wife has a duty not to complain in public.

____ 3. Which sentence reflects most clearly that Adams's letter is a private one?
   A. "He has had recourse to coals; but we cannot get grates made and set."
   B. "Here and there is a small cot, without a glass window, interspersed amongst the forest. . . ."
   C. "Yesterday I returned fifteen visits—but such a place as Georgetown appears—why, our Milton is beautiful."
   D. "It is a beautiful spot, capable of every improvement."

____ 4. Why do you think it is so hard to get wood for the White House fires?
   A. It is hard to find woodcutters because the area is so underpopulated.
   B. It is hard to find woodcutters because everyone in town is a politician.
   C. The staff is afraid that burning wood will turn the White House black.
   D. The distance to the forests is so great.

____ 5. Which of these details is a fact supporting Adams's opinion that the new White House is built "upon a grand and superb scale"?
   A. It is "an establishment very well proportioned to the President's salary."
   B. "The river, which runs up to Alexandria, is in full view of my window."
   C. "To assist us in this great castle, and render less attendance necessary, bells are wholly wanting."
   D. It requires "about thirty servants to attend and keep the apartments in proper order, and perform the ordinary business of the house."

____ 6. What can you infer about Adams's character from the tone and details of her letter?
   A. Wealth and power do not impress her.
   B. She is very loyal to her family and friends.
   C. Comfort is extremely important to her.
   D. She is one to make the best of any situation, no matter how bad.

___ 7. The title *Letters from an American Farmer* suggests that Crèvecoeur's writing is
   A. informal and intimate.
   B. personal but formal.
   C. logical and objective.
   D. complex and ornate.

___ 8. Crèvecoeur's facts about the harshness of everyday European life support his opinion that people can feel little loyalty to a nation that
   A. fails to enable its citizens to live decently.
   B. has recently lost a war.
   C. does not contain citizens from different ethnic and religious backgrounds.
   D. rewards those who own substantial property.

___ 9. What point does Crèvecoeur make by comparing people to plants?
   A. People have no control over their own lives.
   B. Like plants, people die if they are not fed and watered.
   C. To thrive, people need to be nurtured by their country.
   D. People who do not have solid ethnic roots cannot be successful.

___ 10. Crèvecoeur argues that American laws are indulgent, protective, and great. What fact does he use to back up this opinion?
   A. American law protects people from their own misdeeds.
   B. All Americans are allowed to vote.
   C. The law rewards those who work hard with land and freedom.
   D. The government of America is based on the desires of its people.

___ 11. Why is this sentence typical of the style of an epistle: "I could point out to you a family whose grandfather was an Englishman, whose wife was Dutch, whose son married a French woman, and whose present four sons have now four wives of different nations"?
   A. It uses exaggeration.
   B. It backs up its point with evidence.
   C. It contains specific details.
   D. It addresses its reader personally.

___ 12. When Crèvecoeur argues that "Here the rewards of his industry follow with equal steps the progress of his labor," he is appealing to a belief in
   A. human equality.
   B. the importance of technology.
   C. the goodness of human nature.
   D. logical cause and effect.

Vocabulary and Grammar

___ 13. When Adams says that she engaged someone "to *extricate* us out of our difficulty," she means that she hired someone
   A. to set them free from their difficulty.
   B. to counsel them about their difficulty.
   C. to take their minds off their difficulty.
   D. to prove to them that they had no difficulty.

Name _____ Date _____

___ 14. Where could you correctly use semicolons in the following passage?

According to Crèvecoeur, many Europeans suffer from poverty, hunger, and war. He defines an American as someone who, giving up old ways, takes on new ones and becomes part of a new race.

   A. after *who*
   B. after *ways*
   C. after *war*
   D. after *war* and *ways*

Essay

15. Abigail Adams's letter makes us aware of the dramatic contrasts between the appearance of Washington in Adams's time and its appearance today. Write an essay discussing these contrasts, using details from Adams's letter to develop your discussion.

16. Write an essay in which you explain how Abigail Adams's letter provides a clear sense of the undeveloped state of the nation in general at the time the letter was written.

17. Write an essay in which you summarize Crèvecoeur's definition of an American and then explain whether, in your opinion, his definition can still be applied to Americans today.

Name _____ Date _____

Writing About Literature—Unit 2
Evaluate Literary Themes

Prewriting: Formulating a Thesis

Use the chart below to organize your analysis of several authors' references to freedom.

Selection	Reference	Method / Message

Drafting: Presenting Examples

Use the graphic organizer below to organize the support for your essay.

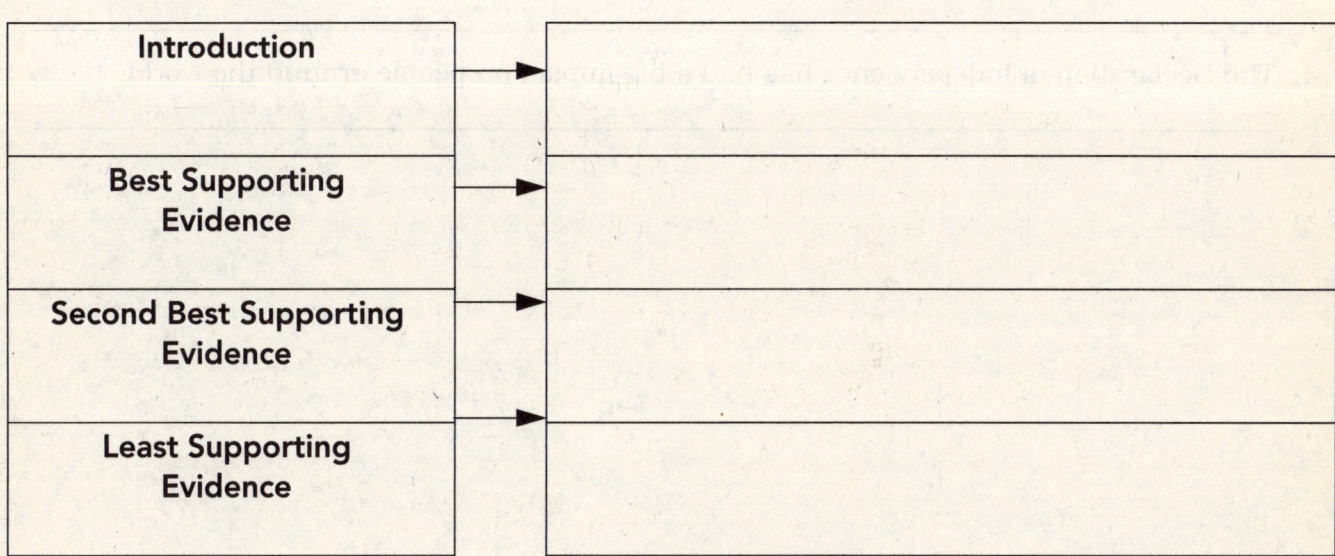

Part of Essay → Examples to Include

- Introduction
- Best Supporting Evidence
- Second Best Supporting Evidence
- Least Supporting Evidence

Unit 2 Resources: A Nation Is Born
© Pearson Education, Inc., publishing as Pearson Prentice Hall. All rights reserved.

Name _____ Date _____

Writing About Literature—Unit 2
Evaluate Literary Themes: Integrating Grammar Skills

Replacing Vague Adjectives

An evaluative essay includes value-laden adjectives such as *effective*, *clear*, and *persuasive*. To make your essay more compelling, replace vague adjectives such as *good* with more precise alternatives. If you have repeated certain adjectives too often, replace them with synonyms.

Vague: Patrick Henry was a *good* speaker.

Precise: Patrick Henry was an *electrifying* speaker.

Identifying Vague Adjectives

A. DIRECTIONS: *In each sentence, underline any vague adjectives.*

1. Thomas Paine's essay *Common Sense* was popular and important in the colonies.
2. Some colonists thought that Paine's ideas were bad and that his personality was awful.
3. Benjamin Franklin was an interesting writer who had a big influence on the Continental Congress.
4. Interesting editorials in colonial newspapers played a big role in inspiring the American Revolution.

Fixing Vague Adjectives

B. DIRECTIONS: *Rewrite each sentence, replacing vague adjectives with vivid, precise ones.*

1. Thomas Paine's *Common Sense* made a strong argument in favor of independence.
   _____

2. In *The Crisis*, Paine offers strong criticism of the Tories who opposed the Revolution.
   _____

3. Thomas Jefferson was a good writer and a good leader.
   _____

4. The Declaration of Independence has had a big impact on people around the world.
   _____

Name _____ Date _____

Writing Workshop—Unit 2
Persuasion: Persuasive Essay

Prewriting: Gathering Details

Use the T-chart below to help you organize the arguments for and against your viewpoint.

Your Essay Topic:

Evidence for your viewpoint	Evidence against your viewpoint

Drafting: Organizing the Essay

Use the chart below to effectively organize the arguments of your persuasive essay.

Interesting introduction	
Your second-strongest argument	
Other less strong arguments	
Present and refute opposing ideas	
Your strongest argument	
Catchy conclusion	

Name _____ Date _____

Writing Workshop—Unit 2
Persuasive Essay: Integrating Grammar Skills

Using Parallelism

Parallel structure is the repeated use of similar ideas in a similar grammatical form. In a persuasive essay, parallelism enhances the power of your language. Parallel expressions help you emphasize your arguments and create a compelling rhythm.

Not Parallel	Philadelphia is famous for *the First Continental Congress, housing the Liberty Bell,* and *publishing the nation's first newspaper.*
Parallel	Philadelphia is famous for *hosting the First Continental Congress, housing the Liberty Bell,* and *publishing the nation's first newspaper.*

Identifying Faulty Parallelism

A. DIRECTIONS: *For each item, circle the word or phrase that is not parallel with the others in the series.*

1. Cell phones provide fun, keeping you safe in an emergency, and convenience.
2. To avoid disturbing the people around you, turn off your cell phone in libraries, when you're going to the movies, and in school.
3. Don't embarrass yourself and others in public by talking too loud, discussing personal issues, or you shouldn't have an argument either.
4. Luxury cell-phone features include cameras, searching the Internet, and e-mail service.

Fixing Faulty Parallelism

B. DIRECTIONS: *Rewrite each sentence so that it uses parallel structures to present a series of ideas.*

1. Until recently, most people saved paper photos in shoeboxes, photo albums, or they bought frames for them.
   _____

2. Today, digital cameras are changing the way people take photos, how they are saved, and share them.
   _____

3. Digital cameras require no film, you have instant pictures, and allow easy sharing.
   _____

4. Digital photos are a good way for a group of people to share memories of a family celebration, a school program, or when you're on the same sports team.
   _____

Name _____ Date _____

Spelling—Unit 2
Proofreading Practice

DIRECTIONS: *Proofread the following passage, looking for 14 misspelled words. Cross out each misspelled word, and write it correctly in the space above.*

Every year, on the Fourth of July, Americans should pause to aknowledge the importance of the Decleration of Indepenance, which was written by Thomas Jefferson. In our observance of our nationel holiday, we should aquaint ourselves with the words of the document that stands at the centre of American ideals. Perhaps no words in history are as inmortal as Jefferson's claim that "all men are created equal."

Jefferson also presented evidence of British responsabilaty for inproper acts that had deprived the colonists of their rights. He objected, for example, to the fact that the British had maned the colonies with armed troops and that they had often baned acts of protest. He argued the impossiblity of accepting such acts of tyranny any longer. Jefferson's words inspired a meagre colonial army to prevail against one of the strongest empires of the time. His words continue to inspire freedom-loving people throughout the world.

Name _____ Date _____

Communications Workshop—Unit 2
Analyze Persuasive Techniques

To help you analyze the effectiveness of each speech's organization and support, answer the questions in the chart below.

Subject of speech: _____

What is the main purpose of the speech?
What evidence is presented?
What proof does the speaker provide that pertains directly to the thesis?
What persuasive language is used?
Which type of persuasive speech did you find most compelling? Why?

Name _____ Date _____

Suggestions for Further Reading—Unit 2

DIRECTIONS: *Think about the books suggested in this unit that you have read. Then, on a separate sheet of paper, answer the discussion questions and take notes for your literature circle.*

The Rights of Man by Thomas Paine

Discussion Paine makes it obvious that an offensive war is not supportable but a defensive war is. Discuss how Paine's ideas of government to make this a logical conclusion.

Connections—Literature Circle Many of Paine's ideas can be seen in our current government. Explore ways in which one of Paine's ideas translates into modern practice.

The Federalist Papers by Alexander Hamilton, James Madison, John Jay

Discussion Discuss whether you think the arguments in No. 23 about the importance of national security are of greater or lesser relevance now than they were in 1787.

Connections—Literature Circle Do you think the checks and balances of the Constitution have worked as planned, or has one of the branches come to overshadow the other two? Support your answer with specific examples from the text.

The Anti-Federalist Papers and the Constitutional Convention Debates edited by Ralph Ketchum

Discussion Many of the antifederalists were concerned about excessive intrusions of a distant central government into citizens' lives. Discuss the current law that you think is the most intrusive, as well as the law that you think is the most helpful.

Connections—Literature Circle Discuss whether you think the antifederalists' concerns about the Constitution were justified in light of the gituation in present-day America. Be specific in your response, developing your opinions with relevant examples from the book.

The Interesting Narrative and Other Writings by Olaudah Equiano

Discussion Discuss Equiano's diction and tone when he describes what happens after he and his crew rescue the eleven men stranded on the boat.

Connections—Literature Circle Discuss Equiano's arguments about why he thinks an Africa free of the slave trade would be beneficial to Great Britain.

Complete Writings by Phillis Wheatley

Discussion What do the poems from "Thoughts on the Works of Providence" to "Niobe in Distress" suggest about life in Wheatley's day?

Connections—Literature Circle In her letter to Obour Tanner, Wheatley observes "how much greater force example is than instruction." Explain whether you agree.

The Autobiography and Other Writings by Benjamin Franklin

Discussion Suggest an even in the book that illustrates one of Franklin's thirteen virtues. Then, discuss which virtue is the most valuable in your life.

Unit 2 Resources: A Nation Is Born
© Pearson Education, Inc., publishing as Pearson Prentice Hall. All rights reserved.

Name _____   Date _____

Unit 2: A Nation Is Born
Benchmark Test 2

MULTIPLE CHOICE

Literary Analysis and Reading Skills *Read the selection. Then, answer the questions that follow.*

> Thus, some tall tree that long hath stood
> The glory of its native wood,
> By storms destroyed, or length of years,
> Demands the tribute of our tears.
>
> from "On the Death of Dr. Benjamin
> Franklin" by Philip Morin Freneau

1. To clarify the meaning of lines 1–4, how might you rephrase them?
   A. A tree representing Franklin has fallen in the woods.
   B. An important person has died and deserves our respect.
   C. If we do not protect our woods, they will be destroyed.
   D. When the elderly die, we should not mourn.

2. From what type of poem does this stanza come?
   A. prose poem
   B. poem of praise
   C. performance poem
   D. nonsense verse

3. What conclusion can you draw about the speaker's feelings toward Benjamin Franklin?
   A. The speaker admires and loves Franklin.
   B. The speaker is indifferent toward Franklin.
   C. The speaker thinks that Franklin helped his country.
   D. The speaker feels as though Franklin was a member of the family.

4. What figure of speech does the following sentence contain?

   The flower lifted its droopy head and drank eagerly.

   A. simile
   B. metaphor
   C. personification
   D. assonance

5. The sentence below is an example of which of the following?

   He that lies down with Dogs, shall rise up with fleas.

   A. advice
   B. aphorism
   C. proverb
   D. monologue

Read the selection. Then, answer the questions that follow.

I was born a slave; but I never knew it till six years of happy childhood had passed away. My father was a carpenter, and considered so intelligent and skilful in his trade, that, when buildings out of the common line were to be erected, he was sent for from long distances, to be head workman. On condition of paying his mistress two hundred dollars a year, and supporting himself, he was allowed to work at his trade, and manage his own affairs. His strongest wish was to purchase his children; but, though he several times offered his hard earnings for that purpose, he never succeeded.

from *Incidents in the Life of a Slave Girl* by Harriet Jacobs

6. Which sentence best summarizes the selection?
   A. Though he was a slave unable to purchase his children, the author's father was a skilled carpenter able to work independently at his trade.
   B. The author never knew she was a slave because her father worked independently as a carpenter even though he had to pay his owner.
   C. The author did not know she was a slave because her father paid his owner $200 so that he could work at his trade and manage his own affairs.
   D. The author's father wanted more than anything else to purchase his children because they were born slaves even though they did not know it.

7. Why does the last sentence evoke strong emotions in the reader?
   A. It points out how hard the father worked.
   B. It points out how much slavery hurts children.
   C. It points out the arbitrary cruelty of slavery.
   D. It points out how much better off some slaves were than others.

8. What makes a slave narrative unique?
   A. It contains a certain amount of fiction.
   B. It contains the daily events in the life of a captive.
   C. It is not a true autobiography.
   D. It gives specific details about the life of a woman.

9. Which of the following is a primary source?
   A. a television documentary about a famous writer
   B. a letter from a famous writer to his mother on her birthday
   C. an invitation from a well-known artist's niece
   D. a fictional narrative about the artist's life

Name _____ Date _____

10. In which of the following situations would it be important to distinguish between fact and opinion?
    A. when you are reading a fantasy novel
    B. when you are studying a poem about death
    C. when you are reading a short story about life in the year 3000
    D. when you are listening to a speech about the environment

11. Which of the following are you most likely to find in a public letter?
    A. a narrative about cooking with imported foods
    B. a poem of affection
    C. an argument for a policy on pets in the park
    D. a description of the day's activities

12. What makes an autobiography different from a history book?
    A. It is told from a personal point of view.
    B. It does not tell about actual events.
    C. It follows chronological order.
    D. It discusses philosophy.

13. Read the following sentence. Then, answer the question that follows.

    I was so thrilled, but I knew that if my family discerned my excitement, they would be afraid.

    In what type of writing would this sentence most likely be found?
    A. public letter
    B. private letter
    C. persuasive appeal
    D. museum placard

Read the following sentence. Then, use the sentence to answer the questions that follow.

If you want a representative who is one of you, who knows your hopes and dreams, who will help you fight oppression, vote for me.

14. What is the purpose of this sentence?
    A. to inform
    B. to entertain
    C. to persuade
    D. to explain

15. If the sentence came from a speech, what would an appropriate audience be?
    A. children at camp
    B. judges of a debate competition
    C. high school students at a rally
    D. voters at a community center

16. Which word from the sentence is a charged word?
    A. representative
    B. hopes
    C. fight
    D. oppression

17. What type of persuasive appeal does the following sentence illustrate?

    Statistics, such as the fact that the average child or teenager watches nearly three hours of television a day, show that it is important to monitor the effects of television-watching on children.
    A. appeal to authority
    B. appeal to reason
    C. appeal to emotion
    D. appeal to public opinion

18. Which of the following speeches would require the most formal diction?
    A. a speech dedicating a new war memorial
    B. a speech introducing a Hall of Fame baseball player
    C. a speech describing an around-the-word adventure
    D. a speech nominating a candidate for student senate

Vocabulary

19. Using your knowledge of the root -vigil-, what does the word *vigilant* mean in the following sentence?

    After the puppy was bitten, he became more vigilant around strange dogs.
    A. hostile
    B. watchful
    C. friendly
    D. hungry

20. What is the meaning of the root word shared by *evidence* and *video*?
    A. to judge
    B. to watch
    C. to see
    D. to record

21. What characteristic does someone have who shows *fidelity*?
    A. intelligence
    B. trustworthiness
    C. laziness
    D. anxiousness

22. What function does the suffix *-ity* perform?
    A. It turns adjectives into adverbs.
    B. It turns adjectives into verbs.
    C. It turns adjectives into pronouns.
    D. It turns adjectives into nouns.

23. The word *revolve* contains the word root *-volv-* and the prefix *re-*. What does the word mean?
    A. loses control
    B. turns repeatedly
    C. gathers speed
    D. becomes overheated

Grammar

24. Which of the following pronouns correctly replaces *Lakeisha* in the sentence below?

    The argument over the granola bar was the first fight I had ever seen between Sarita and Lakeisha.

    A. she
    B. her
    C. they
    D. them

25. Why is the following sentence ungrammatical?

    The instructions were so confusing that she didn't have no idea what to do next.

    A. The subject and verb do not agree in number.
    B. The sentence has a double negative.
    C. The sentence has a misplaced preposition.
    D. The sentence has a split infinitive.

26. Which of the following sentences is written in active voice?
    A. I was frightened by the rising water.
    B. The pamphlets were sent home with the newsletter.
    C. The storm cloud broke open on the children's field trip.
    D. The musician was disappointed by the audience turnout.

27. Which of the following sentences is written in passive voice?
    A. Her laughter makes everyone chuckle.
    B. Sydney spilled her milk for the third time this week.
    C. Louellen plopped down on the couch and sighed.
    D. The memo was written by senior managers.

28. Which of the following sentences correctly uses parallelism?
    A. To get to Omaha, you have to ride a train, catch a bus, or ride in a car.
    B. Louisa was cheerful, creative, courageous, and she had enthusiasm.
    C. The young man in the red shirt ran, jumped, cheered, and collapsed.
    D. My principal was a comedian, an actor, and he also played piano.

29. Which form of the verb *shield* is used in the following sentence?

    The boy sees the ball coming and *shields* himself with his left arm.
    A. perfect tense
    B. past perfect tense
    C. present tense
    D. future tense

30. Where does the semicolon go in the following sentence?

    Juanita says she adores Indian food actually she has never tried any.
    A. between *adores* and *Indian*
    B. between *Indian* and *food*
    C. between *food* and *actually*
    D. between *actually* and *she*

ESSAY

31. You are planning to write an autobiographical account of the year you spent in second grade. How will you begin to gather your ideas? What will you include to make the writing effective? Write a plan for developing your autobiographical account.

32. Think of a historical figure you admire greatly. Jot down a few of the person's major accomplishments. Then, sum up the person's accomplishments for a placard that will accompany the person's portrait in a museum or an inscription that will accompany a monument to that person.

33. Plan a letter to a poet whom you admire. Choose at least one poem that you want to discuss. Select several details from the poem to support your points. Be sure to use language appropriate to your audience.

34. As wonderful as your community may be, no place is perfect. Think of a problem your community faces that you would like to address, and figure out how to solve it. Then, write a proposal to the elected leader of your community in which you present your ideas. Be as persuasive as you can in presenting the need for change and as practical as you can be in making suggestions.

Diagnostic Test 2, p. 2
MULTIPLE CHOICE
1. ANS: B
2. ANS: C
3. ANS: D
4. ANS: C
5. ANS: A
6. ANS: C
7. ANS: A
8. ANS: D
9. ANS: B
10. ANS: D
11. ANS: C
12. ANS: A
13. ANS: D
14. ANS: B
15. ANS: D

Unit 2 Introduction

Names and Terms to Know, p. 5
A. 1. H; 2. D; 3. A; 4. G; 5. C; 6. I; 7. B; 8. E; 9. F

B. Sample Answers
1. The Enlightenment included scientists such as Galileo and Sir Isaac Newton, the philosophers Voltaire and Jean-Jacques Rousseau, and political theorist John Locke.
2. The American Revolution began in Lexington, Massachusetts, under somewhat confusing circumstances. A shot was fired by an unknown person, and a battle followed between the colonists and the British soldiers that continued in Concord and started the Revolutionary War.
3. The Constitution, although it has become a vital document in our nation, did not have everyone's support at the time of its creation. Even Ben Franklin was concerned that it should have been better.
4. *The Federalist* essays were originally written as letters to New York newspapers. They were written for the purpose of getting the legislators in New York to ratify the Constitution.

Focus Questions, p. 6
Sample Answers
1. The French and Indian War was successful for the British, but it depleted their funds. To raise money, they taxed the colonists on a variety of items. Colonists rebelled in both peaceful and violent ways against what they considered to be "taxation without representation," and it was only a matter of time before war would break out.
2. The new country had to deal with a desire to create a centralized government that would still protect the rights of individual freedom. The first document, the Articles of Confederation, promised a "league of friendship," but it was ineffective and replaced by the Constitution. Although the Constitution was eventually ratified, it was marked by controversy and needed to be supplemented by the Bill of Rights.
3. The early leaders of the nation were also great thinkers and writers. Typical forms of political literature included speeches, letters in newspapers, and broadsides that could be posted all over for everyone to read. Leaders such as Ben Franklin wrote literature that has lasted through the ages, such as his *Autobiography*. In addition, the other writers of the time wrote poetry about their experiences (such as the slave Phillis Wheatley) or impressions of the new nation (such as Michel-Guillaume Crèvecoeur) that reflected the political environment.

from *The Autobiography* and from *Poor Richard's Almanack* by Benjamin Franklin

Vocabulary Warm-up Exercises, p. 8
A.
1. conferred
2. enumerations
3. posterity
4. eradicate
5. relapses
6. trifling
7. faulty
8. practicable

B. Sample Answers
1. An artist who publishes her autobiography—a life story written by the person who lived the life—wrote it herself.
2. Yes, the witness is guessing because a speculative account includes speculation, that is, guesswork.
3. Yes, because sensibly means reasonably or appropriately.
4. Yes, if the seats are allotted equally, they are distributed equally.
5. A subsequent bill would be a bill received following the purchase.
6. You might praise a benevolent woman for acts of charity and generosity.
7. An attack that is unremitting (that is, relentless) does not grow weaker.
8. An incorrigible coward does not plan to ever change or correct his cowardice.

Reading Warm-up A, p. 9

Sample Answers

1. (essential); Students may describe a wide variety of *trifling* experiences, such as crossing the street, phoning a friend, or looking out the window.
2. (lists); In a yearbook, you might find *enumerations* of class members, team members, and faculty members.
3. published in a great variety of languages; Putting a computer in the hands of every person on the planet is not *practicable*.
4. (gave); The PTA *conferred* an award on my mother for extra service.
5. not enough for the witness to have seen the crime; Students might tell of buying a *faulty* CD or riding a *faulty* bike.
6. (completely eliminate); Students may say that people should *eradicate* poverty or ignorance.
7. get sick again; My sister and I thought we were over the flu, but we both had *relapses*.
8. (generations, we); We all hope that *posterity* will remember our best intentions and greatest accomplishments.

Reading Warm-up B, p. 10

Sample Answers

1. writing the story of one's own life; Students may cite the *autobiography* of an athlete, celebrity, artist, or virtually anyone.
2. (clearly, perfect combination of passion and reason); Acting *sensibly* now will prevent a great deal of trouble later.
3. assigned; Students may note that they are *allotted* forty minutes for class.
4. (fact and truth); *Speculative* statements may be useful when a scientist is trying to explain a phenomenon or when a detective is trying to solve a mystery.
5. wave after wave; A synonym for *unremitting* is *relentless*.
6. (generous); Students may consider giving money to a stranger or volunteering with a charity to be *benevolent* acts.
7. (stubborn); He is an *incorrigible* liar; he never tells the truth.
8. that come later; Students may note that, *subsequent* to the assignment, they plan to have a snack, watch TV, or go to sleep.

Literary Analysis: Autobiography, p. 11

Sample Responses

1. At the beginning of his attempts at moral perfection, Franklin is confident that he can succeed. He is also determined and willing to try.
2. Franklin is surprised that success eludes him.
3. Franklin is confident that a week's time will be sufficient to cure himself of a particular bad habit.
4. Franklin is surprised that moral perfection is harder to achieve than he had thought.
5. Franklin tells this amusing story as a way of letting himself be satisfied with less than perfection.
6. Franklin decides that not being perfect would make his life easier since people often hate or envy their perfect friends.

Reading Strategy: Draw Conclusions, p. 12

Sample Responses

Conclusion:

1. Franklin was a hard-working and diligent man.
2. Franklin did not reach the perfection he wanted to attain.

Supporting details and reasons:

1. Working on a "bold and arduous project"; designs methodical plan for improving thirteen different virtues; focuses on one virtue at a time and works on them over a period of years.
2. Admits that the task will be difficult and notes his trouble with order: "My scheme of *Order* gave me the most trouble . . . In truth, I found myself incorrigible with respect to *Order*; and now I am grown old, and my memory bad, I feel very sensibly the want of it."

Vocabulary Builder, p. 13

A. Sample Responses

1. being in the state of remaining awake to watch or observe; watchful; observant
2. the state of being excessively awake to watch or observe; too watchful; excessively observant

B. 1. C; 2. E; 3. H; 4. G; 5. D; 6. A; 7. B; 8. F

C. 1. B; 2. C; 3. D; 4. A

Grammar and Style: Pronoun Case, p. 14

Students should underline subjective pronouns and circle objective pronouns.

A.
1. Objective Pronouns: it, him
2. Subjective Pronoun: he
3. Subjective Pronoun: He; Objective Pronoun: it
4. Subjective Pronoun: We; Objective Pronoun: it
5. Subjective Pronoun: I; Objective Pronoun: it

B. 1. I; 2. me; 3. we; 4. they; 5. he; 6. she; 7. him; 8. her; 9. me; 10. he

Enrichment: Multiple Careers, p. 17

Suggested Responses

A. Responses will vary. Franklin's thirteen virtues are temperance, silence, order, resolution, frugality, industry, sincerity, justice, moderation, cleanliness, tranquillity, chastity, and humility. Of these, students will probably list order, resolution, industry, and sincerity most often. Allow students to explain and defend their choices.

B. Responses will depend on the career students choose and may include technical skills or specific areas of education. For example, students who choose the career of diplomat may mention knowledge of one or more foreign languages and cultures as well as personal qualities such as tact and loyalty. Students who choose the career of writer may list computer or word-processing skills and knowledge of English grammar and mechanics. Students who choose the career of scientist may list general knowledge in math and sciences as well as specific knowledge of a particular scientific field.

Selection Test A, p. 18
Critical Reading

1. ANS: A	DIF: Easy	OBJ: Literary Analysis
2. ANS: C	DIF: Easy	OBJ: Literary Analysis
3. ANS: A	DIF: Easy	OBJ: Comprehension
4. ANS: C	DIF: Easy	OBJ: Comprehension
5. ANS: D	DIF: Easy	OBJ: Reading Strategy
6. ANS: B	DIF: Easy	OBJ: Comprehension
7. ANS: B	DIF: Easy	OBJ: Interpretation
8. ANS: C	DIF: Easy	OBJ: Literary Analysis
9. ANS: A	DIF: Easy	OBJ: Reading Strategy
10. ANS: B	DIF: Easy	OBJ: Interpretation
11. ANS: B	DIF: Easy	OBJ: Reading Strategy

Vocabulary and Grammar

12. ANS: C	DIF: Easy	OBJ: Vocabulary
13. ANS: A	DIF: Easy	OBJ: Grammar

Essay

14. Students should describe which quality they might work on themselves to become better people.
    Difficulty: *Easy*
    Objective: *Essay*

15. Students may say that Poor Richard is suggesting that people take their time in giving their friendship to someone, by seeing whether the person is truthful, does his or her share of maintaining the friendship, and so on. Having accepted someone as a friend, the aphorism then suggests that people should be slow to end a friendship.
    Difficulty: *Easy*
    Objective: *Essay*

Selection Test B, p. 21
Critical Reading

1. ANS: C	DIF: Easy	OBJ: Comprehension
2. ANS: B	DIF: Easy	OBJ: Comprehension
3. ANS: A	DIF: Average	OBJ: Interpretation
4. ANS: B	DIF: Average	OBJ: Interpretation
5. ANS: A	DIF: Challenging	OBJ: Literary Analysis
6. ANS: D	DIF: Average	OBJ: Literary Analysis
7. ANS: D	DIF: Easy	OBJ: Literary Analysis
8. ANS: B	DIF: Easy	OBJ: Reading Strategy
9. ANS: C	DIF: Average	OBJ: Reading Strategy
10. ANS: B	DIF: Challenging	OBJ: Reading Strategy
11. ANS: A	DIF: Average	OBJ: Interpretation
12. ANS: C	DIF: Easy	OBJ: Comprehension

Vocabulary and Grammar

13. ANS: A	DIF: Easy	OBJ: Vocabulary
14. ANS: C	DIF: Average	OBJ: Vocabulary
15. ANS: C	DIF: Easy	OBJ: Grammar
16. ANS: D	DIF: Average	OBJ: Grammar

Essay

17. Students should realize that *The Autobiography* is written from the author's point of view and therefore may be biased, while an impartial reporter's work would probably be less biased. Phrases and sentences from the selection might be rewritten as those of an outside observer; for example, "for something, that pretended to be reason, was every now and then suggesting to me that such extreme nicety as I exacted of myself might be a kind of foppery in morals, which, if it were known, would make me ridiculous" might be rewritten as "Franklin was concerned that people would think he was foolish for trying to achieve perfection."
    Difficulty: *Easy*
    Objective: *Essay*

18. Students may respond either way as long as they support their positions with details from the selection. Students who support the statement may say that at one point Franklin felt that perfection was an admirable trait and that he would thus admire the trait in others. Students who reject the statement may point out that Franklin felt frustrated with himself for not being able to master the virtue of order and thus may feel envy for someone who did achieve the virtue.
    Difficulty: *Average*
    Objective: *Essay*

19. Students may take either position as long as it is supported by their interpretation of the aphorism and other details in their essays. Some students may interpret the aphorism strictly—any activity that is not productive is squandering time. Others may interpret it more loosely—wasting time means different things to different people; what one person considers wasting time may bring fulfillment to another, and vice versa. Students' positions will also depend on the value they place on leisure time.
    Difficulty: *Challenging*
    Objective: *Essay*

From the Scholar's Desk

William L. Andrews Introduces *The Interesting Narrative of the Life of Olaudah Equiano* by Olaudah Equiano p. 24

1. It is astonishing that history has preserved almost no firsthand accounts of the Middle Passage. This fact makes Equiano's narrative a rare, detailed report.
2. In composing the narrative, Equiano would almost inevitably have to have relived his suffering and the anguish of others.
3. The first stop is the ship's suffocating hold, where conditions are "loathsome." The "human cargo" is forced to stand for most of the transatlantic voyage. On the deck, Africans are dying of the illnesses they have contracted in the hold. The European crew merely watches and waits, indifferent to the captives' suffering.
4. They sympathize with the ten-year-old African narrator, feeling his shock and dread. They are alienated from the brutal whites.
5. According to Andrews, Equiano's peek into the quadrant gives him a glimpse of an unimagined world and arms him with a resilience and inquisitiveness that will allow him to survive. Evaluations of Andrews's claim will vary.

William L. Andrews

Listening and Viewing, p. 25

Sample answers and guidelines for evaluation:

Segment 1: William L. Andrews first became interested in studying African American history and culture by growing up in the segregated South; African Americans were part of his world but also separated from his world, which made him curious to learn more about their culture. Andrews acts as a middle man by pointing out the relevance of these nineteenth-century writings to people today.

Segment 2: Olaudah Equiano was a slave who purchased his own freedom and became a shrewd businessman. He wrote a book about his experiences coming to America on a slave ship and overcoming tremendous odds; this book became the foundation for all slave narratives. Students may answer that slave narratives are firsthand accounts written by slaves or former slaves about their experiences. Students may suggest that slave narratives are important to society because they offer a personal, intimate account of significant historical events that occurred during the nineteenth century, and they provide a different perspective than traditional history books.

Segment 3: William L. Andrews researches primary sources when writing about historical figures of the past because he wants to learn as much as possible about the person, reading documents written by people that were personally and directly involved with the subject. Students may suggest that they could offer insights into the writer's life and personality that may provide further understanding of the description of events in the narratives, and could also verify factual details.

Segment 4: Slave narratives often tell stories that have the "common denominators" of emotion, hardship, and humanity that all readers can relate to in their own lives. Students may answer that readers can learn from Equiano's narrative because it shows the diversity that exists in the world and allows the reader a greater perspective for interaction in today's global world.

from *The Interesting Narrative of the Life of Olaudah Equiano* by Olaudah Equiano

Vocabulary Warm-up Exercises, p. 27

A.
1. climate
2. intolerably
3. confined
4. dejected
5. persuaded
6. unmercifully
7. suffocated
8. render

B. Sample Answers
1. False; Having copious amounts of work means you have much to do.
2. False; If your condition is aggravated, it is made worse.
3. True; Inseparable means always together.
4. False; To undergo treatment is to let a doctor take care of you.
5. True; Custody includes responsibility for someone or something.
6. False; To pacify is to soothe, not fight and destroy.
7. True; When you gratify a desire, you satisfy it.
8. False; Avarice is greed, the opposite of generosity.

Reading Warm-up A, p. 28

Sample Answers
1. (unacceptably); Students may describe an *intolerably* disruptive phone conversation in a movie theater or an *intolerably* steep rise in prices.
2. depressed; To avoid feeling *dejected*, people may listen to music, go out with friends, sing, laugh, or whistle.
3. (un); The boss kept piling on more and more work *unmercifully*.
4. (flourishing landscapes, hot Southern); Students may describe their local *climate* as temperate, hot, dry, cold, wet, or with another appropriate weather-related term.
5. small rooms; Someone may be *confined* in an office, jail, or hospital.
6. (close quarters); To be *suffocated* is to be unable to breathe.

7. make; Students may *render* the school day better by making it shorter.
8. (use the paintings as a curriculum resource); I saw an athlete I admire in an ad for a sports drink that *persuaded* me to run out and buy some.

Reading Warm-up B, p. 29
Sample Answers
1. endure; Students may mention having to *undergo* listening to a long lecture or making a trip to the dentist.
2. (made worse); Antonyms of *aggravated* include *irritated* and *exacerbated*.
3. greed; The gambler looked at the money with wide eyes, and his *avarice* was his downfall.
4. (their desire); To *gratify* is to satisfy, especially a craving.
5. torn apart; *Inseparable* things might include two friends or a cowboy and his horse.
6. (many); The hills stretched into the distance, covered with *copious* amounts of grass.
7. (were in charge of); I had *custody* of the children while their parents went to the movies.
8. soothe; To *pacify* an angry customer, a salesperson may suggest an exchange or a refund.

Literary Analysis: Slave Narratives, p. 30
Sample Responses
1. Examples of oppression include being lied to about the ship's destination, the arbitrary changing of Equiano's name by his master, being struck for refusing to answer to a name that is not his choice.
2. Equiano's response to the change in his name was different in that he protested the change instead of merely giving in to oppression as he had done on his voyage from Africa. Perhaps Equiano's greater maturity or better understanding of his situation account for the difference.
3. Equiano may have felt that Olaudah is his African name to be reserved for the time when he was once again free.
4. Gustavus I was the son of a nobleman of the Vasa family and the first king of an independent Sweden. The name was an appropriate choice because Equiano was also the son of a leader—a tribal elder in the powerful kingdom of Benin in Africa.

Reading Strategy: Summarizing, p. 31
A. Sample Responses
Main Idea: The traders mistreated their captives. Key Supporting Details: tossed fish overboard rather than feed it to the captives; when captives tried to get fish, they were flogged
Main Idea: Equiano, in spite of the hardship, finds time to think about sailing on the ocean. Key Supporting Details: mentions flying fishes; first sees quadrant used
Main Idea: The captives are landed at Barbados and sold into slavery. Key Supporting Details: merchants and planters inspect captives; captives bewildered, terrified; old slaves let captives know what will happen—they won't be eaten but will be put to work

B. Sample Response
Equiano and his fellow captives are crammed aboard a ship under terrible conditions: crowded, smelly, disease-ridden. Their captors treat them cruelly, and many slaves perish. Despite the hardships, Equiano does take note of his first experience of sailing the ocean, mentioning such things as flying fish and the use of a quadrant. When he and his fellow slaves arrive in Barbados and are inspected by prospective buyers, they are quite terrified until older slaves explain that they will not be eaten but put to work.

Vocabulary Builder, p. 32
A. 1. a tape for viewing (as opposed to listening only)
2. easily seen
B. 1. B; 2. C; 3. E; 4. F; 5. D; 6. A
C. 1. avarice; 2. loathsome; 3. improvident;
4. pestilential; 5. pacify; 6. copious

Grammar and Style: Active and Passive Voice, p. 33
A. 1. A; Possible response: All the cargo was taken into the ship.
2. A; Possible response: The scene was turned into almost inconceivable horror.
3. P; Possible response: Two of the wretches drowned themselves.
B. Sample Responses
1. Slave traders kidnapped Equiano and his sister from their home in West Africa.
2. No change necessary; the specific identity of the performers of the action is not important.
3. No change necessary; the general merchant identity of the performer of the action is clear from the opening prepositional phrase, and more specific information is unknown and unimportant.

Enrichment: Film Portrayals of the Slave Trade, p. 36
Suggested Responses
Students should demonstrate a knowledge of the film of their choice and support their answers with details of the setting, dialogue, events, and characterization in the film.

Selection Test A, p. 37
Critical Reading

1. ANS: B	DIF: Easy	OBJ: Literary Analysis
2. ANS: A	DIF: Easy	OBJ: Comprehension
3. ANS: C	DIF: Easy	OBJ: Interpretation
4. ANS: C	DIF: Easy	OBJ: Literary Analysis
5. ANS: A	DIF: Easy	OBJ: Reading Strategy

6. ANS: B	DIF: Easy	OBJ: Reading Strategy
7. ANS: C	DIF: Easy	OBJ: Interpretation
8. ANS: D	DIF: Easy	OBJ: Interpretation
9. ANS: A	DIF: Easy	OBJ: Comprehension
10. ANS: A	DIF: Easy	OBJ: Comprehension
11. ANS: D	DIF: Easy	OBJ: Reading Strategy
12. ANS: B	DIF: Easy	OBJ: Comprehension
13. ANS: A	DIF: Easy	OBJ: Interpretation

Vocabulary and Grammar

| 14. ANS: B | DIF: Easy | OBJ: Vocabulary |
| 15. ANS: B | DIF: Easy | OBJ: Grammar |

Essay

16. Students' essays may mention that by overloading the ship, the slavers made sure that even with the deaths, there would be enough slaves who lived through the journey to make them a profit at the other end.
    Difficulty: *Easy*
    Objective: *Essay*

17. Students' essays should reflect that Equiano would have had to learn to both read and write a completely new language. He would have had to have a very good memory to recall the events of the ocean crossing. He would also have needed a strong wish for freedom to earn enough money to free himself and go on to write his autobiography.
    Difficulty: *Easy*
    Objective: *Essay*

Selection Test B, p. 40

Critical Reading

1. ANS: D	DIF: Easy	OBJ: Literary Analysis
2. ANS: A	DIF: Average	OBJ: Literary Analysis
3. ANS: B	DIF: Challenging	OBJ: Interpretation
4. ANS: B	DIF: Average	OBJ: Literary Analysis
5. ANS: D	DIF: Average	OBJ: Interpretation
6. ANS: A	DIF: Average	OBJ: Interpretation
7. ANS: C	DIF: Average	OBJ: Comprehension
8. ANS: C	DIF: Easy	OBJ: Comprehension
9. ANS: B	DIF: Average	OBJ: Interpretation
10. ANS: C	DIF: Challenging	OBJ: Reading Strategy
11. ANS: A	DIF: Easy	OBJ: Interpretation
12. ANS: C	DIF: Average	OBJ: Reading Strategy
13. ANS: A	DIF: Challenging	OBJ: Interpretation

Vocabulary and Grammar

14. ANS: C	DIF: Easy	OBJ: Vocabulary
15. ANS: B	DIF: Easy	OBJ: Vocabulary
16. ANS: A	DIF: Average	OBJ: Vocabulary
17. ANS: B	DIF: Average	OBJ: Grammar

Essay

18. While students' descriptions of their personal responses to the shipboard captivity will differ, they should be based on details contained in the narrative and their writing in total should provide an adequate summary.
    Difficulty: *Easy*
    Objective: *Essay*

19. Students should cite details showing the hardships of the slaves and the shock and horror these details would most likely inspire in readers. They may also discuss how reading the selection would help humanize slaves for white readers by showing the narrator to be a sensitive, intelligent human being forced to face inhuman conditions. Among the details students may suggest that abolitionists use are those revealing the horrors of the slave crossings, the harshness of the slave traders, and the cruelties of the slave market.
    Difficulty: *Average*
    Objective: *Essay*

20. Students may point out that Equiano's writing shows his obvious intelligence, that his eye for detail and interest in the quadrant and flying fish show his curiosity, that his feelings for his fellow captives show his compassion, and that his condemnation of the treatment of the captives shows his sense of justice.
    Difficulty: *Challenging*
    Objective: *Essay*

The Declaration of Independence
by Thomas Jefferson
from *The Crisis, Number 1* by Thomas Paine

Vocabulary Warm-up Exercises, p. 44

A.
1. pursuit
2. invariably
3. inevitably
4. absolute
5. impels
6. entitle
7. burden
8. rejoice

B. Sample Answers
1. No, to be in compliance with the regulations is to follow them.
2. No, if workers are obstructing the street, they are blocking it.
3. No, depriving yourself means not allowing yourself to do something.

4. A <u>consolation</u> prize gives comfort to someone who has not won.
5. No, it does not show good judgment, so it is not <u>prudent</u>.
6. No, to <u>abolish</u> a law is to do away with it.
7. Yes, <u>tyranny</u> allows a ruler to do whatever he or she wants.
8. Yes, if you are <u>deriving</u> pleasure from something, it is delighting you.

Reading Warm-up A, p. 45

Sample Answers

1. (almost always); Students may say that they *invariably* play sports in the afternoon, go shopping on the weekend, or watch tv in the evening.
2. seeking; Students may say the *pursuit* of happiness involves searching for or working for security, prosperity, love, and satisfaction.
3. (have the right to); Being older does not *entitle* you to treat others with disrespect.
4. urged; Students may say that love of freedom and respect for democratic principles should *impel* every American to vote.
5. (complete); Students may consider virtually any song an *absolute* masterpiece.
6. laid on the shoulders, weight, bear; Students may consider a *burden* a household chore, a financial problem, or some other responsibility.
7. (could not be prevented); *Inevitably* may be defined as taking place in a way that cannot be avoided or stopped.
8. happiness and satisfaction; Students may mention that they *rejoice* when their sports team wins or when they find some money.

Reading Warm-up B, p. 46

Sample Answers

1. obtain; Students may say that the tools they most often use for *deriving* information are books, the Internet, newspapers, and television.
2. (unjust and willful rule); A person who engages in *tyranny* is a *tyrant*.
3. careful, good judgment; The employee felt that he had to complain, but he decided to be *prudent* and keep quiet.
4. (do away with); Students might like to *abolish* injustice, college entrance exams, or restrictions on downloading music.
5. go along with; Most athletes understand that *compliance* with all league regulations ensures fair play for everyone.
6. (preventing); Not having enough science credits is seriously *obstructing* my path toward a degree.
7. (not having or using); *Depriving* myself of those particular foods has really taken a lot of self-control.
8. comfort; When my friend's dog died, I took her to the pet store, and she found some *consolation* in getting a new dog.

Literary Analysis: Persuasion, p. 47

Sample Responses

1. **Emotional and logical appeals.** Paine uses the emotionally charged words *tyranny, hell,* and *glorious,* and he places himself on an equal basis with his audience by using the pronouns *us* and *we;* he also uses common-sense comparisons and cause-and-effect relationships in a logical chain of seemingly reasonable observations.
2. **Emotional appeal.** Paine places himself on an intimate level with his audience and compliments them as he calls them to action.
3. **Emotional and logical appeals.** Paine stresses the justness of the colonial cause by depicting it as a defensive war and uses the negatively charged words *thief, kills,* and *threatens* in a personal analogy with which most of his audience can identify, an analogy that appeals to his audience's sense of self-preservation and family responsibility. At the same time, he opens with a seemingly reasonable refutation of his distaste for an offensive war, and he then leads the audience through a logical chain of reasoning that summarizes his argument.

Reading Strategy: Recognizing and Evaluating Charged Words, p. 48

Sample Responses

1. abuses, usurpations, despotism: These negative words emphasize the negative behavior of the British monarch and help arouse colonial indignation at his mistreatment.
2. wholesome, necessary, public good: These positive words stress the idea that the colonial position is perfectly justified and nobly motivated.
3. oppressions, humble: The words, one negative and one positive, stress the contrast between Britain's insensitivity and the colonies' laudable behavior.
4. tyranny, hell: These negative words emphasize the negative behavior of the British monarch and help arouse colonial indignation at his mistreatment.
5. warm ardor, friend: These positive words stress the nobility of the colonial cause and appeal to colonial loyalties.

Vocabulary Builder, p. 49

A. Sample Responses

1. having faith in herself; trusting herself
2. faithfulness
3. in trust
4. trust

B. 1. D; 2. B; 3. A; 4. C

Grammar and Style: Parallelism, p. 50

A. 1. Single underscore: that all men are created equal; that they are endowed by their creator with certain inalienable rights; that among these are life, liberty and the pursuit of happiness

   Double underscore: life, liberty, pursuit of happiness

2. Single underscore: to alter, to abolish, to institute new government

    Double underscore: laying its foundation on such principles, organizing its power in such form

    Triple underscore: safety, happiness

3. Single underscore: free, independent

    Double undescore: levy war, conclude peace, contract alliances, establish commerce, do all other acts and things

B. Sample Responses

1. The delegates pledge their lives, their fortunes, and their sacred honor.
2. Jefferson criticizes the king for taking away colonial charters, abolishing colonial laws, and altering the colonial government.

Enrichment: Local Newspaper Editorial, p. 53

Suggested Responses

Responses will vary. Students who take Paine's approach should use charged words and symbols that appeal to readers' emotions. Students who take Jefferson's approach should present a logical argument in calmer tones, with ample supporting evidence. In either case, editorials should make clear what actions readers are to take or changes readers are to support and should provide some rationale for those actions or changes.

Selection Test A, p. 54

Critical Reading

#	ANS	DIF	OBJ
1.	C	Easy	Literary Analysis
2.	C	Easy	Reading Strategy
3.	B	Easy	Interpretation
4.	C	Easy	Comprehension
5.	C	Easy	Interpretation
6.	D	Easy	Comprehension
7.	C	Easy	Reading Strategy
8.	A	Easy	Literary Analysis
9.	A	Easy	Literary Analysis
10.	B	Easy	Reading Strategy
11.	D	Easy	Comprehension

Vocabulary and Grammar

#	ANS	DIF	OBJ
12.	B	Easy	Vocabulary
13.	C	Easy	Grammar

Essay

14. Students' essays may suggest that colonists were still very close to England and had family members in England. They also did not want to be alone as a new nation. Finally, to many colonists, the fight for independence was not only frightening, it was treasonous.

Difficulty: *Easy*

Objective: *Essay*

15. Students' essays should reflect the basic meaning of Paine's words, which might be paraphrased in this way: "If a task is hard to do, we feel much more victorious if we succeed." Students may suggest that Paine said these things not only because he believed them, but also because he was writing to convince many readers to go into a struggle that would be long and hard, and with no guarantee of success.

Selection Test B, p. 57

Critical Reading

#	ANS	DIF	OBJ
1.	B	Average	Interpretation
2.	A	Easy	Reading Strategy
3.	C	Average	Reading Strategy
4.	D	Easy	Comprehension
5.	D	Easy	Interpretation
6.	D	Average	Comprehension
7.	A	Average	Interpretation
8.	B	Challenging	Interpretation
9.	A	Average	Literary Analysis
10.	C	Challenging	Literary Analysis
11.	C	Average	Interpretation
12.	C	Easy	Reading Strategy
13.	A	Challenging	Reading Strategy

Vocabulary and Grammar

#	ANS	DIF	OBJ
14.	A	Easy	Grammar
15.	B	Average	Vocabulary

Essay

16. Students might mention one or more of the following: anger, because the document reminds them of the wrongs done by the king; fear, because the Declaration is treason and means more war; sorrow, because life will change and long-standing ties with Britain will break; uncertainty, because no one knows the outcome of events; hope, because things could get better; pride, because the colonies have taken a stand and expressed it in strong but reasonable terms; joy, because the colonies are throwing off tyranny; and patriotism, because people are taking the first steps toward becoming an independent nation.

Difficulty: *Easy*

Objective: *Essay*

17. Students may say Paine's essay would have raised spirits because of its expression of thanks and love for those fighting; the assurance that God will give them victory; the nobility of their cause (peace and freedom for their children); the justice of the war (a defensive war against tyranny); the rallying cry for support from everyone; and the praise of those who follow principles and stand firm in difficult times. Some students may say that the

essay would not raise spirits because of its emphasis on difficult conflict with the possibility of death; on giving up a safe, peaceful course; and on the idea that the rewards are deferred to the next generation.

Difficulty: *Average*

Objective: *Essay*

18. Students should recognize that Jefferson uses parallelism quite effectively in the Declaration of Independence to help create a structured argument in favor of the separation of the colonies from Britain and to emphasize the key elements of that argument. For example, Jefferson repeatedly uses the word *that* to stress each of the rights of all people. In the heart of the Declaration, in which Jefferson lists the many ways in which the king of Great Britain has used his power over the colonists in a tyrannical way, Jefferson highlights his accusations by beginning each one with the words "He has" and a past participle.

Difficulty: *Challenging*

Objective: *Essay*

"An Hymn to the Evening" and "To His Excellency, General Washington"
by Phillis Wheatley

Vocabulary Warm-up Exercises, p. 61

A.
1. soothe
2. realms
3. majestic
4. proceed
5. implore
6. deforms
7. refined
8. destined

B. **Sample Answers**
1. The yoga teacher <u>exhales</u> slowly whiles she stretches.
2. The customers came to the refreshment stands in <u>surges</u>, before each movie.
3. Looking down from the window of the jet, the ocean appeared <u>boundless</u>.
4. The museum had an entire section devoted to books on <u>martial</u> subjects.
5. She drove for three hours to get to the concert and was so <u>drowsy</u> when it began, she had to struggle to stay awake.
6. In order to <u>prevail</u> over his opponent, the congressman campaigned heavily.
7. Jockeys wear colorful silk <u>array</u> to make their horses stand out during a race.

Reading Warm-up A, p. 62
Sample Answers
1. (its massive wingspan and ability to soar to great heights); A redwood tree is *majestic* because it has grandeur and stateliness.
2. *Proceed* means to continue with something, especially after an interruption.
3. (in the wild and in captivity); *realms* are areas
4. (pollution thins and <u>deforms</u> the shell of the eagle's egg); *deforms* means to disfigure or distort the appearance or function of something.
5. (the government); *implore* means to entreat, to beg for.
6. ([the bell was . . .] rung when the Continental Congress signed the Declaration of Independence in 1776. Because the bell was linked to that moment in history); *Destined* means assigned for a certain purpose.
7. (Because of the many people . . . died defending it); *refined* means polite and free for any coarseness.
8. (The gesture is meant to show gratitude, ie. Presenting the flag to the next of kin); *soothe* means to bring comfort and relief.

Reading Warm-up B, p. 63
Sample Answers
1. (he concentrated on systems like the post office, libraries, and fire rescue squads); *martial* means pertaining to war
2. Fine <u>array</u> in Colonial times meant a silk vest and waistcoat with silver buttons, a ruffled shirt with lace cuffs, velvet pants and high heeled shoes. Plain clothes would be made of cotton or wool, and would be worn with boots.
3. Franklin's imagination was considered <u>boundless</u> because it was used in so many areas. *Boundless* means without limits.
4. (bifocal glasses, daylight savings time, the odometer, lightening rods); *prevail* means to persist in spite of obstacles or changes.
5. (so much heat); *exhale* means to breathe out
6. Often people tending open flames became <u>sleepy</u> and failed to notice sparks that could set their homes ablaze.
7. (electricity that formed lightening); *surges* are sudden increases
8. After a certain number of rotations, the odometer triggered bells that could be heard <u>ringing</u> in the postal wagon.

Literary Analysis: Personification, p. 64
Sample Responses
1. Earth is personified as a mother who gave birth to the American colonists.
2. The nations of the world are personified as people capable of gazing at scenes and being unfamiliar with them.
3. The speaker's pen is personified as the writer of the lines; some students may also note that the poet's Muse, whom she addresses directly, is a personification of the abstract idea of poetic inspiration, further personified as being capable of bowing.
4. Autumn is personified as a monarch enjoying a golden reign.
5. A century is personified as something having a destiny.

Reading Strategy: Clarify Meaning, p. 65

Sample Responses

1. I write about Columbia's scenes of glorious struggles.
2. While freedom's cause disturbs her anxious breast.
3. As when the wind spoils heaven's fair face.
4. Where the unfurled flag waves high in [the] air.
5. Shall I repeat their praise to Washington?
6. Hear every tongue beg for your protective aid!
7. The scent of the blooming spring blows out from the west wind's wings.
8. The streams ripple softly.
9. And their combined music floats through the air.
10. So may our breasts glow with every virtue.

Vocabulary Builder, p. 66

A. Sample Responses
  1. to claim again; to bring back to good condition
  2. to leap back; to recover

B. 1. heavenly; 2. shining; 3. favorable; 4. flowing back; 5. thoughtful; 6. calm; 7. rod or staff

C. 1. A; 2. D

Grammar and Style: Subject and Verb Agreement, p. 67

A. Students should underline the subject once and the verb twice and then circle whether the subject and verb are singular or plural.
  1. Subject: she; Verb: flashes; SINGULAR
  2. Subject: nations; Verb: gaze; PLURAL
  3. Subject: charms and graces; Verb: rise; PLURAL
  4. Subject: surges; Verb: beat; PLURAL
  5. Subject: they; Verb: seek; PLURAL
  6. Subject: Britannia; Verb: droops; SINGULAR
  7. Subject: incense; Verb: exhales; SINGULAR
  8. Subject: dyes; Verb: are spread; PLURAL
  9. Subject: west; Verb: glories; SINGULAR
  10. Subject: scepter; Verb: seals; SINGULAR

B. 1. comes; 2. were; 3. was; 4. represents; 5. appears; 6. describes; 7. praise

Enrichment: Fine Art, p. 70

Suggested Responses

1. Responses will vary. Students should note that the painting shows an inscription stating that George Washington is first in war and that the foot of Liberty is standing on a crown, symbolizing that to win freedom, Americans had to defeat the British king; the statue shows Washington holding a sword up and riding as if he is leading people to battle.
2. Responses will vary. Students who choose the statue may explain that it shows Washington upright and riding forward, or proceeding, as directed in Wheatley's lines. Students who choose the painting may explain that in it the depiction of Liberty placing a crown on Washington's head reflects the crown in Wheatley's lines and that the inscription in the painting stresses the "great Chief" and the virtues mentioned in Wheatley's lines.
3. Responses will vary, but students should note that the painting is predominately red, white, and blue, the colors of the American flag, showing the artist's patriotic attitude and/or view of Washington as a symbol of the nation. Students may also mention that Washington's head is gray, making it resemble a monument carved in marble, further conveying the idea that Washington is more a symbol than a person.
4. Responses will vary. Students should include and/or thoughtfully describe the symbolism of the images, materials, and colors in their piece of visual art.

Selection Test A, p. 71

Critical Reading

1. ANS: A	DIF: Easy	OBJ: Literary Analysis
2. ANS: C	DIF: Easy	OBJ: Reading
3. ANS: B	DIF: Easy	OBJ: Comprehension
4. ANS: A	DIF: Easy	OBJ: Literary Analysis
5. ANS: C	DIF: Easy	OBJ: Literary Analysis
6. ANS: C	DIF: Easy	OBJ: Reading
7. ANS: B	DIF: Easy	OBJ: Interpretation
8. ANS: B	DIF: Easy	OBJ: Reading
9. ANS: D	DIF: Easy	OBJ: Comprehension
10. ANS: B	DIF: Easy	OBJ: Reading
11. ANS: C	DIF: Easy	OBJ: Interpretation

Vocabulary and Grammar

12. ANS: D	DIF: Easy	OBJ: Vocabulary
13. ANS: C	DIF: Easy	OBJ: Vocabulary
14. ANS: C	DIF: Easy	OBJ: Grammar

Essay

15. Wheatley experiences evening and sunset as beautiful and peaceful. She is clearly outdoors observing the sky and acutely aware of sensory impressions. Many students will note that, because most Americans live in cities or suburbs, few experience the peaceful, relaxing qualities of evening that Wheatley describes in her poem. To support their opinions, students should refer to specific details and examples from the poem and from modern life.

Difficulty: *Easy*
Objective: *Essay*

16. Guidelines: Evaluate students' essays for clarity and coherence. They should state their opinion clearly at the outset of the essay and then support their opinion with examples from the texts. Students' essays should discuss both Wheatley's themes and her style.

Difficulty: *Easy*
Objective: *Essay*

Selection Test B, p. 74
Critical Reading

1. ANS: B	DIF: Challenging	OBJ: Comprehension
2. ANS: C	DIF: Average	OBJ: Comprehension
3. ANS: C	DIF: Challenging	OBJ: Literary Analysis
4. ANS: C	DIF: Average	OBJ: Interpretation
5. ANS: A	DIF: Average	OBJ: Interpretation
6. ANS: C	DIF: Easy	OBJ: Literary Analysis
7. ANS: D	DIF: Average	OBJ: Literary Analysis
8. ANS: A	DIF: Average	OBJ: Literary Analysis
9. ANS: B	DIF: Average	OBJ: Reading Strategy
10. ANS: A	DIF: Average	OBJ: Reading Strategy
11. ANS: A	DIF: Average	OBJ: Reading Strategy

Vocabulary and Grammar

12. ANS: A	DIF: Challenging	OBJ: Vocabulary
13. ANS: C	DIF: Average	OBJ: Vocabulary
14. ANS: B	DIF: Average	OBJ: Vocabulary
15. ANS: D	DIF: Average	OBJ: Grammar
16. ANS: D	DIF: Average	OBJ: Grammar
17. ANS: B	DIF: Challenging	OBJ: Grammar

Essay

18. Students may have logical reasons for choosing either day or night as Wheatley's preferred choice. Students who believe she liked day better may support their opinion with descriptions of the rain, spring, birds, and sunset. Students who believe she liked night better may support their opinion by pointing out that the title is dedicated to the evening and that the poem contains descriptions of sable curtains, restful sleep, and renewal from sleep, as well as the message that the tranquillity of night strengthens people for the day.
Difficulty: *Easy*
Objective: *Essay*

19. Students will probably feel that Wheatley was very patriotic. These students may mention, among other things, Wheatley's portrayal of America as a goddess, her praise for America's champion General Washington, her picture of a fierce and faithful American army, her depiction of America as strong and "heaven-defended," and her view of America as a model for other countries.
Difficulty: *Average*
Objective: *Essay*

20. Most students will likely equate General Washington with America itself. They may compare specific details praising Columbia, an embodiment of America, with details praising Washington himself. They may point out that Wheatley portrays Americans as "heaven-defended" and Washington as someone with "virtue on his side." Students may also discuss the title, suggesting that the poem is really written to all Americans, even though it is specifically addressed to General Washington.
Difficulty: *Challenging*
Objective: *Essay*

"Speech in the Virginia Convention"
by Patrick Henry
"Speech in the Convention"
by Benjamin Franklin

Vocabulary Warm-up Exercises, p. 78

A. 1. sentiments
2. conduct
3. reserve
4. reconciled
5. cope
6. invincible
7. avert
8. revere

B. Sample Answers
1. The group spurned the newcomer and refused to accept him.
2. The guard was vigilant and paid close attention to his job.
3. Our group performed with great efficiency, wasting no time or energy.
4. Troubled with irresolution, she took no action.
5. This arduous task is so difficult you will have to make a great effort.
6. We have plenty of implements, so we have tools to do the job.
7. He infected our computers with an insidious virus that no one knew about.
8. This summer, I plan to indulge in adventure novels and read a lot of them.

Reading Warm-up A, p. 79
Sample Answers
1. (speeches, decisions, acts, and attitudes); Appropriate *conduct* in a classroom includes paying attention, participating in the lesson, and respecting other people's opinions.
2. admire; Students may say they *revere* someone for his or her character, talents, or extraordinary accomplishments.
3. (much stronger); You may feel *invincible*, but you can be beaten.
4. thoughts and feelings; Students may say that their *sentiments* about American literature include admiration, respect, love, and curiosity.

5. (full and free); I wanted to tell the principal how angry I really felt, but I spoke with *reserve* during the entire meeting.
6. prepared drafts and worked out compromises; Students may say that people would want to *avert* a standstill in order to continue to make progress and move toward a goal.
7. (opposing points of view); The critic *reconciled* his negative comments about the novel with substantial praise for it.
8. create procedures, backtrack, reconsider issues; On the way to school each morning, our bus has to *cope* with the traffic that clogs the roads.

Reading Warm-up B, p. 80
Sample Answers
1. treacherous; Students may say that they find *insidious* the advertising that lures them to buy products they don't really need or want.
2. (building, shaping, maintaining); Writing *implements* include pen, pencil, chalk, felt marker, and computer.
3. disagreed; He *spurned* all the attempts by his friends to persuade him to dress more fashionably.
4. (hesitating); Frozen with *irresolution*, he did not move to the left or the right, and the shopping cart banged into him.
5. no unnecessary provisions or wasted words; In business, *efficiency* is essential because time is money.
6. (great struggle); My car broke down and I had to make an *arduous* trek across a deserted landscape to reach a little town.
7. (abuses of power); As she increased in maturity, she learned not to *indulge* in the fits of temper that had driven away her friends.
8. watching over; My science experiment demanded that I remain *vigilant* all night, observing carefully to detect any changes.

Literary Analysis: Speeches, p. 81
Sample Responses
Restatement: "If we wish to be free. If we wish to preserve inviolate those inestimable privileges for which we have so long been contending"; "there is no peace. The war is actually begun. The next gale that sweeps from the north will bring to our ears the clash of resounding arms! Our brethren are already in the field!"
Repetition: "Let it come, I repeat, let it come"; the word *slavery* throughout; the word *peace* in the last paragraph
Parallelism: "We have petitioned; we have remonstrated; we have supplicated"; "Our petitions have been slighted; our remonstrances have produced additional violence and insult; our supplications have been disregarded"; "give me liberty or give me death!"
Rhetorical Questions: "Is this the part of wise men, engaged in a great and arduous struggle for liberty?" "Are fleets and armies necessary to a work of love and reconciliation?" "Can gentlemen assign any other possible motive for it?" "And what have we to oppose to them?" "Shall we try argument?"

Reading Strategy: Evaluating Persuasive Appeals, p. 82
Sample Responses
1. **Reason:** The line suggests that listeners act in the present based on past experience. It makes a generalization that it asks listeners to apply to a specific case.
2. **Reason and emotion:** While terms such as *martial array* and *submission* are charged with emotion, the basic argument presented in these sentences appeals to reason.
3. **Reason and emotion:** Henry presents a great deal of evidence and then draws a logical conclusion from it, but he also uses charged words like *violence, insult, supplication,* and *spurned.*
4. **Emotion:** The remark appeals to listeners' religious faith by implying that the colonists have God on their side, and it depicts the rebels as loyal friends of the audience and of liberty.
5. **Reason and emotion:** Henry offers solid reasons to support the Revolution, but he also uses emotional exclamations and repetition as well as poetic language that imbues nobility in the colonists' struggle, such as *gale from the north* and *clash of resounding arms.*

Vocabulary Builder, p. 83
A. 1. believability; 2. complexity; 3. flexibility; 4. infallibility; 5. creativity
B. 1. synonyms; 2. antonyms; 3. synonyms; 4. antonyms; 5. antonyms; 6. synonyms; 7. synonyms; 8. antonyms; 9. antonyms; 10. antonyms

Grammar and Style: Double Negatives, p. 84
A. Students should underline the following negative words and contractions in items 1–5 and 7 but should underline nothing in item 6. 1. never, no 2. n't, none 3. n't, nothing 7. n't, no 5. n't, no 4. hardly, no one
B. **Sample Responses**
1. I'll never go to any Badgers games again.
2. Why won't you go to any of those Badgers games?
3. The Badgers don't know anything about basketball! (or: The Badgers know nothing about basketball!)
4. That star player allows hardly anyone to get in his way.
5. They play as if they haven't got any sense, (or: They play as if they have no sense.)
6. Correct
7. Well, maybe it just wouldn't have done any good.

Enrichment: Persuasion, p. 87

Suggested Responses

Students' ads should include a rhetorical question, perhaps right at the start, and should include at least one example of each of the three other persuasive techniques, using them to hammer home key ideas in the ad. Students should recognize that radio ads have a listening audience, not a viewing or reading one, and may incorporate sound effects and other devices that appeal to the audience's sense of hearing.

Selection Test A, p. 88

Critical Reading

1. ANS: B	DIF: Easy	OBJ: Comprehension
2. ANS: C	DIF: Easy	OBJ: Literary Analysis
3. ANS: D	DIF: Easy	OBJ: Interpretation
4. ANS: C	DIF: Easy	OBJ: Comprehension
5. ANS: A	DIF: Easy	OBJ: Reading Strategy
6. ANS: C	DIF: Easy	OBJ: Interpretation
7. ANS: D	DIF: Easy	OBJ: Literary Analysis
8. ANS: B	DIF: Easy	OBJ: Reading Strategy
9. ANS: A	DIF: Easy	OBJ: Comprehension
10. ANS: D	DIF: Easy	OBJ: Literary Analysis
11. ANS: B	DIF: Easy	OBJ: Interpretation

Vocabulary and Grammar

12. ANS: A	DIF: Easy	OBJ: Vocabulary
13. ANS: A	DIF: Easy	OBJ: Grammar

Essay

14. Students' essays may point out that he might have been speaking these words to symbolize how important the struggle for independence from Britain was for the colonists. For those who believe he meant the words literally, they might point out that the likelihood of war with Great Britain was high and that Henry and other patriots were determined to free themselves from England.
    Difficulty: *Easy*
    Objective: *Essay*

15. Students' essays should reflect that people who have lived a long life often realize that they cannot have perfection. Students may give examples from their own experiences, in which they hope for something to change or hope to accomplish something perfectly on the first try, and are cautioned by older people that this is rarely the case.
    Difficulty: *Easy*
    Objective: *Essay*

Selection Test B, p. 91

Critical Reading

1. ANS: C	DIF: Easy	OBJ: Comprehension
2. ANS: D	DIF: Easy	OBJ: Comprehension
3. ANS: D	DIF: Average	OBJ: Reading Strategy
4. ANS: C	DIF: Easy	OBJ: Literary Analysis
5. ANS: B	DIF: Average	OBJ: Literary Analysis
6. ANS: C	DIF: Challenging	OBJ: Reading Strategy
7. ANS: C	DIF: Challenging	OBJ: Reading Strategy
8. ANS: B	DIF: Average	OBJ: Reading Strategy
9. ANS: D	DIF: Average	OBJ: Comprehension
10. ANS: C	DIF: Easy	OBJ: Literary Analysis
11. ANS: A	DIF: Challenging	OBJ: Interpretation

Vocabulary and Grammar

12. ANS: D	DIF: Challenging	OBJ: Vocabulary
13. ANS: B	DIF: Easy	OBJ: Grammar
14. ANS: B	DIF: Average	OBJ: Grammar
15. ANS: A	DIF: Average	OBJ: Vocabulary

Essay

16. Students who are stirred by the speech and find it effective, moving, and convincing will probably cite Henry's emotion-charged view that the stake is freedom or slavery and that liberty is worthy of great sacrifice and his more logical depiction of British actions as seemingly bent on subjugation and of the colonists as having exhausted all peaceful means of settling the conflict. Students who are less moved or convinced by the speech may find it excessive in its expression, suspiciously one-sided and warlike, and they may wonder if it is a triumph of rhetoric over reason.
    Difficulty: *Easy*
    Objective: *Essay*

17. Students should mention that Franklin has reservations about the new Constitution but is not sure if he is right about them. He urges unanimous support of the Constitution on the grounds that it may well be the best Constitution possible, given the large number of people collaborating on it, and it is better to present unanimous front that will make the people of the new nation more enthusiastic about accepting it.
    Difficulty: *Average*
    Objective: *Essay*

18. Students may include some or all of these points along with the rhetorical device, such as rhetorical question, Henry uses to stress each one. Answering those who

object out of hope for peace, Henry replies that the past actions of the British leave no room for hope—nor do their present actions of a military buildup. Answering those who say other means than war should be tried, Henry replies that the colonists have been trying these means for ten years, to no avail. To those who say the colonies are too weak, Henry says that they will never be stronger than they are now and that they have a holy cause—liberty—that justifies their actions even if they are defeated.
Difficulty: *Challenging*
Objective: *Essay*

"Letter to Her Daughter from the New White House" by Abigail Adams
from *Letters from an American Farmer* by Michel-Guillaume Jean de Crèvecoeur

Vocabulary Warm-up Exercises, p. 95

A.
1. metamorphosis
2. inconvenience
3. continual
4. compact
5. ample
6. extensive
7. establishment
8. confer

B. Sample Answers
1. No, if you extricate yourself from trouble, you are no longer caught in it.
2. No, an indulgent supervisor would not enforce the rules strictly and would allow people to do things their own way.
3. A family worried about subsistence would be concerned about the basic necessities of food, clothing, and shelter.
4. Yes, if taking part is voluntary, people may choose whether or not they wish to participate.
5. If a runner has expended his energy, he has used it all up and has none left for the rest of the race.
6. A theater with two hundred seats can accommodate, or fit, two hundred people.
7. If the maple trees were interspersed, they were scattered, not bunched together.
8. A man suffering from penury does not have enough money to relieve his extreme poverty.

Reading Warm-up A, p. 96
Sample Answers
1. (little); Things that may be described as *compact* include a car, a cell phone, a poem, and a community.
2. changing its form; Students may describe the *metamorphosis* of a caterpillar into a butterfly or that of a person undergoing a fashion makeover.
3. (building, mansion, House); In this *establishment*, all guests are expected to wear proper attire.
4. broad; Synonyms for *ample* include *spacious*, *abundant*, and *hefty*.
5. (long, reaching out to great expanses); Students may describe a landscape or seascape, an investigation, or a report as *extensive*.
6. the fact that many people already owned the land he planned to build on; An *inconvenience* is a fact, event, or situation that gets in the way of achieving a goal or making progress. It is usually minor, and often irritating.
7. (keeps cropping up); New and better sci-fi movies are a *continual* delight.
8. grant; I would be honored if they were to *confer* the Nobel Prize on me.

Reading Warm-up B, p. 97
Sample Answers
1. entanglements; Students may say that they would *extricate* a bird from a wire fence by carefully freeing its wings and feet and letting it go.
2. (every effort); Every available resource should be *expended* to fight poverty, including food, seeds, tools, education, and economic aid.
3. made their own choices; *Volunteer* is formed from the same root as *voluntary*.
4. (Native American methods); My friend had to stay in town overnight, and we were able to *accommodate* her in the spare bedroom.
5. If something is *interspersed*, it is scattered or positioned in many different places among other things; In the photo, the models with red shirts were *interspersed* among the models with yellow shirts.
6. (avoided [because they] made small profits); Antonyms for *penury* include *wealth*, *riches*, and *affluence*.
7. For their own *subsistence*, the farmers needed enough food to feed their families, adequate clothing for the seasons, and a reliable shelter.
8. careless, undisciplined; My two puppies had missed me during the day, so I felt *indulgent* and let them jump all over me.

Literary Analysis: Private and Public Letters (Epistles), p. 98
1. E; 2. PL; 3. E; 4. PL; 5. PL; 6. E; 7. E

Reading Strategy: Distinguish Between Fact and Opinion, p. 99
Sample Responses
Opinion: During the ten years that began in 1774, Abigail's life was extraordinarily difficult. **Facts That Support It:** spent most of those years apart from husband; raised four young children in that time; managed family farm in his absence

Opinion: Meanwhile John had become one of the infant American nation's most influential political figures. **Facts That Support It:** member of the Continental Congress; second President of the United States

Opinion: Abigail . . . had a voice of some importance in the new nation. **Facts That Support It:** early American advocate of women's rights; once admonished husband to "Remember the ladies. Do not put unlimited power in the hands of husbands"; also said, "If particular care and attention is not paid to the ladies, we are determined to foment rebellion, and will not be bound by any laws in which we have no voice or representation"

Vocabulary Builder, p. 100

A. 1. A; 2. C; 3. C; 4. A
B. 1. despotic; 2. penury; 3. agues; 4. extricate; 5. asylum; 6. subsistence

Grammar and Style: Semicolons, p. 101

A. 1. E; 2. C; 3. E; 4. C
B.
1. The White House seems superbly designed; its excellent situation offers a fine view of the Potomac River.
2. The oval drawing room will be beautiful when it is completed; even unfinished, it is handsome.
3. There are forests all around, but no one will cut wood; there is coal, but no grates to burn it in.
4. America offers asylum to the poor of Europe; here, people can farm their own land.

Enrichment: Writing a Business Letter, p. 104

Suggested Responses
Students' letters should follow correct business-letter conventions and be carefully proofread to avoid errors in grammar, usage, and mechanics. Encourage students to type their letters or to keyboard and print them on a computer.

Selection Test A, p. 105

Critical Reading

1. ANS: C	DIF: Easy	OBJ: Reading Strategy
2. ANS: B	DIF: Easy	OBJ: Reading Strategy
3. ANS: B	DIF: Easy	OBJ: Comprehension
4. ANS: C	DIF: Easy	OBJ: Literary Analysis
5. ANS: A	DIF: Easy	OBJ: Interpretation
6. ANS: C	DIF: Easy	OBJ: Interpretation
7. ANS: A	DIF: Easy	OBJ: Reading Strategy
8. ANS: B	DIF: Easy	OBJ: Literary Analysis
9. ANS: B	DIF: Easy	OBJ: Comprehension
10. ANS: B	DIF: Easy	OBJ: Literary Analysis
11. ANS: D	DIF: Easy	OBJ: Comprehension

Vocabulary and Grammar

12. ANS: A	DIF: Easy	OBJ: Vocabulary
13. ANS: C	DIF: Easy	OBJ: Grammar

Essay

14. Students' essays may reflect that Adams was in her own way a pioneer as the first First Lady. She faced her new tasks with good humor: helping develop a new capital city in the wilderness; making a mostly unfinished house livable; keeping her negative thoughts to herself; and keeping in touch with her children.
   Difficulty: *Easy*
   Objective: *Essay*

15. Students' essays should reflect that a melting pot is generally thought to be the place where people of many nations, cultures, and religions form a new country. Examples include the fact that people can become citizens, own land, become prosperous, and so on, or that one law applies to all.
   Difficulty: *Easy*
   Objective: *Essay*

Selection Test B, p. 108

Critical Reading

1. ANS: B	DIF: Easy	OBJ: Comprehension
2. ANS: D	DIF: Challenging	OBJ: Interpretation
3. ANS: C	DIF: Average	OBJ: Literary Analysis
4. ANS: A	DIF: Average	OBJ: Interpretation
5. ANS: D	DIF: Challenging	OBJ: Reading Strategy
6. ANS: D	DIF: Average	OBJ: Interpretation
7. ANS: A	DIF: Average	OBJ: Literary Analysis
8. ANS: A	DIF: Challenging	OBJ: Reading Strategy
9. ANS: C	DIF: Average	OBJ: Comprehension
10. ANS: C	DIF: Average	OBJ: Reading Strategy
11. ANS: D	DIF: Easy	OBJ: Literary Analysis
12. ANS: D	DIF: Challenging	OBJ: Interpretation

Vocabulary and Grammar

13. ANS: A	DIF: Easy	OBJ: Vocabulary
14. ANS: C	DIF: Average	OBJ: Grammar

Essay

15. Students should cite details from the letter and compare them to such things as the present-day city's roads, buildings, and monuments; its teeming populace and hectic pace; and the modern conveniences that make travel and communication easier.
   Difficulty: *Easy*
   Objective: *Essay*

16. Students should recognize that Adams' casual description of getting lost on the way to Washington and her statement that there is nothing between the capital and Baltimore but woods give a strong immediate picture of how undeveloped the country is. Other details add to this sense as the letter progresses: the capital is a city in name only; small cottages without glass windows are scattered in the forest; there are few humans to be seen; obtaining simple amenities in the nation's capital is difficult; many buildings are unfinished, the President's home in particular.
Difficulty: *Average*
Objective: *Essay*

17. Students should mention such points as these in their summaries: According to Crèvecoeur, an American is an immigrant or a descendant of immigrants; he is melted into a new race; he has left his past culture behind and adopted a new one; he is a free and full citizen of his new country; he will entertain new ideas and form new opinions; he will love his new country because, unlike his old, it rewards his labors and its laws protect him; and he will work hard, because work is in his self-interest here. Students who feel that the definition applies today may say that people of different backgrounds (no longer just Europeans) are still melted into a new American people, that Americans are still patriotic because they have freedom and a good life here, and that Americans generally enjoy a high standard of living. Those who disagree may feel that America's different racial and ethnic groups have not all melted into a new people, that economic disparities have little or nothing to do with hard work or lack of it, or that many Western European countries now have less poverty than America has.
Difficulty: *Challenging*
Objective: *Essay*

Writing About Literature—Unit 2

Evaluate Literary Themes: Integrating Grammar Skills, p. 112

A.
1. popular, important
2. bad, awful
3. interesting, big
4. Interesting, big

B. Sample revisions.
1. Thomas Paine's *Common Sense* made a *passionate* argument in favor of independence.
2. In *The Crisis*, Paine offers *harsh* criticism of the Tories who opposed the Revolution.
3. Thomas Jefferson was a *brilliant* writer and an *inspiring* leader.
4. The Declaration of Independence has had a *dramatic* impact on people around the world.

Writing Workshop—Unit 2

Persuasive Essay: Integrating Grammar Skills, p. 114

A.
1. keeping you safe in an emergency
2. when you're going to the movies
3. you shouldn't have an argument either
4. searching the Internet

B.
1. Until recently, most people saved paper photos in shoeboxes, photo albums, or frames.
2. Today, digital cameras are changing the way people take photos, save them, and share them.
3. Digital cameras require no film, provide instant pictures, and allow easy sharing.
4. Digital photos are a good way for a group of people to share memories of a family celebration, school program, or a sports event.

Spelling—Unit 2

Proofreading Practice, p. 115

1. acknowledge; 2. Declaration; 3. Independence;
4. national; 5. acquaint; 6. center; 7. immortal;
8. evidence; 9. responsibility; 10. improper;
11. manned; 12. banned; 13. impossibility; 14. meager

Benchmark Test 2, p. 118

MULTIPLE CHOICE
1. ANS: B
2. ANS: B
3. ANS: A
4. ANS: C
5. ANS: A
6. ANS: A
7. ANS: C
8. ANS: B
9. ANS: B
10. ANS: D
11. ANS: C
12. ANS: A
13. ANS: B
14. ANS: C
15. ANS: D
16. ANS: D
17. ANS: B
18. ANS: A
19. ANS: B

20. ANS: C
21. ANS: B
22. ANS: D
23. ANS: B
24. ANS: B
25. ANS: B
26. ANS: C
27. ANS: D
28. ANS: C
29. ANS: C
30. ANS: C

ESSAY

31. Students should demonstrate that they would brainstorm events and details from their second-grade school year. They should include specific details that help the reader to understand what happened and why it was important.

32. Students' placards or inscriptions should accurately sum up the person's major accomplishments.

33. Students should demonstrate an ability to plan a letter. They should use examples from a poem to support their main idea. They should also include language appropriate to their audience.

34. Students' proposals should clearly present both a problem and a solution. Proposals should include persuasive language. Suggestions should make sense.